The fo

Many Realtors might put this down as too elementary, but I wish all my clients would review the simple steps provided here so they could learn to be an effective part of the teamwork it takes to fulfill their dreams. This book has the exact things most buyers and sellers need to know but are afraid to ask.

—John Foltz, President, Realty Executives

This book is a wonderful road map for the ever-confusing world of real estate. It's like having your own personal coach in a box.

—Melissa Giovagnoli, Author, best-selling book, *Networlding: Building Relationships and Opportunities for Success* and *How to Grow a Great Business and Power Network*

The real estate world is constantly changing, so anyone who is even considering buying [or selling] property of any kind should first get a copy of this easy-to-read and straightforward book. [It] demonstrates how valuable a good real estate professional can be—and further—how to select the right one. Smart real estate agents will also read the book to ensure their [clients] are receiving the service and the expertise they deserve.

—Dave Liniger, Co-founder and Chairman of RE/MAX

This book should be required reading for all Realtors® and for anyone serious about real estate.

—Peter J. McLaughlin, author of *CatchFire: A Seven Step Program to Ignite Energy, Defuse Stress and Power Boost Your Performance*

I read your book and I think it is eminently readable. That's one thing most such publications intended for the public fail to be. There is a lot of good information in it that consumers can benefit from.

—Edwin J. Ricketts, Deputy
Commissioner of the Arizona
Department of Real Estate

. . . In life it seems you don't get what you deserve, you get what you negotiate, and *How to Make Your REALTOR® Get You the Best Deal* gives you the necessary tools it takes to be in the best possible position to negotiate in real estate. My hat is off to Jenny, Ken, and their national consortium.

—Mike Barnett, VP Technology of
Internet Crusade (an organization
providing communication training to
Realtors® nationwide)

In this book . . . Several profoundly successful real estate agents have provided a simple guide through the often dark and confusing waters of homebuying or selling. They demonstrate the impact of recent changes in the law and how those changes can affect the quality of representation one receives. Read this book and you will learn how to screen, select, and then use your Realtor® in a way that *Gets You the Best Deal.*

—Steve Largent, U.S. Congressional
Representative, Oklahoma

This is a ground-breaking work for home sellers. It is not only a quick read, but it puts in layman's terms the language of real estate. This book will do more to empower the homeseller than anything else in print. I strongly recommend you buy this book before you even consider putting your home on the market.

—Michael E. Houtari, Corporate
Attorney

Get the Best Deal When Selling Your Home

Southeast Michigan Edition

Get the Best Deal When Selling Your Home

Southeast Michigan Edition

by Wynne Achatz,
Doug and Kathie Whitehouse,
and
Ken Deshaies

Gabriel Publications

Gabriel Publications
14340 Addison St. #101
Sherman Oaks, California 91423
Visit our website at www.gabrielbooks.com
Or call: (800) 940-2622

Get The Best Deal When Selling Your Home, Southeast Michigan Edition
Wynne Achatz, Doug and Kathie Whitehouse, and Ken Deshaies
ISBN-13: 978-1-891689-73-4
ISBN-10: 1-891689-73-8
Library of Congress Catalog Card Number: 2006922066
Typography: SDS Design, info@sds-design.com
Cover Design: Dale Schroeder, SDS Design
Editors: David Robman, Kate Shaffar, and Nina M. Hickey
Publisher: Gabriel Publications, Simon Rawlinson, V.P.
Distributed by: Partners Publishers Group
Printed in the United States of America.

Contents

Selling Your Home: The Basics

Buying Your Next Home

Acknowledgments by Wynne Achatz

After **Ken Deshaies** and I did the *Buyer Book,* we started talking about a *Seller Book*. Ken jumped right on it and got started. Then other real estate practitioners from around the country jumped on board as well. **Doug Whitehouse** and I opted in right away for the Southeastern Michigan Edition. Because of leadership duties to perform and family commitments, we had to delay our book for two years. We want to thank Ken and **Rennie Gabriel** for their patience.

Since Ken and I did the Michigan buyer book, a lot has changed. This is to again acknowledge all those in that book and to add to those acknowledgments for this book. I am so happy to have worked with Doug Whitehouse. Thank you to Doug's daughter, **Samantha**, our attorney and overseer for this project.

My family is still around me, inspiring me and urging me on. My dad and business partner since 1978, **Gordon Westrick**, passed March 3, 2003. I still look to him as an angel on my shoulder. He is around all the time getting me through the tough times today's real estate market has presented. Many of the skills I have now are attributed to his "tough love" attitude. On my first day in the business, Dad had this to say, "Business was not given, it was earned. Educating yourself, taking classes, and attending seminars are important to grow a real estate career. Giving back to the real estate community is next. After that comes your business. You will know what to do. Attend meetings. Meet the important leaders in the industry and watch what they do. Become a leader. Become a mentor for others. Business will come. Learn by the actions of your fellow Realtors®."

My daughter **Jayme** has blessed us with our first grandchild, **Koen Rolla Lanker**. She and her husband live in Ann Arbor, Michigan. **Jacob** has gotten his "dream" Harley and works in Canton, Michigan. My mom, **Shirlee Westrick**, still working as a commercial real estate broker in Vero Beach Florida, compiles the homes magazine for several counties. She gives me lots of incentive. She never stops.

Judy Vaughn is still one of my assistants. **Dick Anderson** is semi-retired, but is there with guidance when needed. We have some new players on the TEAM. **Jim Achatz**, Accredited Buyer Agent, intends to follow in my footsteps and someday will be TEAM leader. **Deb Dudas** has become my assistant and right arm. **Rod Papin**, retired police chief from Marine City, is my newest TEAM member. He is steadfast and always on top of things. The Algonac office has changed locations. We are located across from Farmer Jack's near the Algonac Boat Access at 2215 Pointe Tremble. The Marine City office is still in the same location.

Diana Maxwell and I are still active in the community. The CyberStars™ are flourishing and I am still mentoring with **Allen F. Hainge**, industry leader in technology growth. My website designer and good friend, **Sandy Teller**, www.sizzlingstudios.com, is the best in website design—definitely keeping me fresh in that arena. According to *Crain's Business Report*, Real Estate One, Inc. is still #1 in Michigan's real estate sales for over 12 years. **Stuart Elsea** offers so much support to his sales team and franchise offices.

This book is dedicated to the growth of my team and the real estate profession in Michigan.

"To give real service you must add something which cannot be bought or measured with money, and that is sincerity and integrity."

—Donald A. Adams

Acknowledgments by Doug Whitehouse

First, I'd like to acknowledge my wife, **Kathie**. Without her, a career in real estate would not have been possible. Shortly after I started my career, she joined me and we became partners in business as well as partners in life. Both partnerships are the best part of my life.

To our daughter **Samantha** and our son **Bill** who both understood the time it took to get a career started. Both of our children were licensed as soon as they were of legal age and helped to build our business. Samantha, a graduate of the University of Michigan and Georgetown University Law Center, practices corporate, securities and finance law in Chicago at Mayer, Brown Rowe & Maw LLP. Bill, a graduate of Michigan State University, currently works in the field of substance abuse therapy.

Being coauthors of the Southeast Michigan edition of *Get the Best Deal When Selling Your Home* was a joint effort of Doug, Kathie, **Wynne Achatz**, and **Ken Deshaies**. We want to express our gratitude and acknowledge those who have inspired us and helped us achieve success.

This book is a tribute to what we consider to be the most rewarding career we could have chosen—real estate. We say a heartfelt thank you to all of our customers and clients for choosing us to serve them. This book is also an opportunity to give something of value to future customers and clients and we are delighted with the opportunity to do so.

There are many people in the Realtor® organization that have helped us over the years. Thanks to our business partner at Hannett, Wilson & Whitehouse LLC, Realtors®, **Kathy Wilson**. A huge thanks to **Linda Cook**, CRS, president of the Michigan Chapter Charter, and a great mentor, for introducing us to our first state convention and showing us the real meaning of what it is to be a Realtor®. We would like to thank the CEO of the South Oakland County Board of REALTORS®, **Maurice Richards**, for helping us to see the value of being involved and nudging us into leadership. It is our involvement at the local board level that helped me to see the value of expanding that involvement to the state and national levels.

A thank you to the Michigan Association of REALTORS® (MAR), particularly to our friends, **Bill Martin, Rob Campau**, and **Kathie Feldpausch**. We have learned much from each other and we truly appreciate your exceptional knowledge of the real estate industry and your willingness to share that knowledge with the membership and us. We'd also like to express our appreciation to the leadership of MAR for allowing Doug to serve as their state president in 2005.

To the Women's Council of REALTORS®, for allowing Kathie to serve as a chapter president, national governor, and as state president in 1999. These experiences enhanced our lives greatly.

To the National Association of REALTORS®, 1.2 million members strong this year, for allowing Doug to serve as a national director and as vice chairman of the Business Issues Committee in 2007. It has been an honor to serve.

We hope this book will be a valuable tool to Michigan real estate buyers. We are happy to see you achieve the American dream of home ownership.

Acknowledgments by Ken Deshaies

There are those without whom this book would not have been written, and they deserve more than the recognition given here. Their faith in me, at times, exceeded my own.

My publisher, **Rennie Gabriel**, and I have formed a partnership of ideas that has done several things. My first book, *How to Make Your Realtor® Get You the Best Deal,* has been much more successful than either of us ever imagined. As a consequence, we have both been able to bring a semblance of understanding and self-help to thousands of consumers across this great land. We have also enabled dozens of Realtors® to participate in getting out their message. In the process, we have become great friends and cohorts. Not everyone will agree with our methods, but we have not necessarily been seeking agreement. What we have done, I would hope, is to empower people on both sides of the real estate purchasing process along with the professionals who work with and represent them.

I must thank my good friend, a fellow Realtor® and e-PRO, **Mollie Wasserman**. Mollie is a true pioneer in the area of real estate and the Internet, and we are truly fortunate that she was willing to provide a special chapter for us on this topic. This is a very important subject in today's real estate transactions, and we urge all of our readers to make sure they are prepared to deal with the benefits and limitations of the Internet.

Davida Sims and **David Robman** contributed so much to this manuscript, and their efforts are more than appreciated.

Allen Hainge is the founder of the CyberStars™, an elite group of Realtors® from around the country and abroad who not only can prove experiential success with the use of technology, but have also agreed to be teaching professionals with Allen. Allen welcomed me with open arms into this wonderful organization several years ago, and he has become a good friend and mentor ever since.

John Beldock, founder of EcoBroker™ International, a school for training real estate professionals about energy efficient homes, has provided valuable contributions to this book.

Thanks to the hundreds of clients with whom my wife, **Mary**, and I have worked with through the years, and who have provided the fodder and the inspiration for this book. So many of them have become good friends in the process that our family is huge in its abundance.

Patricia McDade, founder and inspirational leader of the Entrepreneurial Edge, provided the initial kick in the proverbial rear to get me to do over that which I'd procrastinated for so long.

"You don't end up in the grave. You end up in the hearts of the people you have touched."

Disclaimer

We've tried, we really have. We have attempted to ensure that everything said here is accurate and relevant. But laws change, circumstances vary, home prices and interest rates change, and there is always the possibility for error. There may be mistakes, both typographical and in content, and the information was current only up to the printing date. Using the guidance offered here, along with your selection of a competent real estate professional, you should feel confident in purchasing or selling real estate. This text should be used only as a general guide and not as the ultimate source of real estate information. If your situation is complicated by any of a myriad of factors, such as the property being a business, farm, or ranch, or if it has soil, septic tank, well, or title problems, we recommend you consult with a Realtor® who specializes in that area. We are not providing any accounting, legal, or tax advice in this book. We recommend that you hire an attorney or other appropriate professional who can assist with the specifics involved in any legal or tax matter. The purpose of this book is to educate and entertain. The publisher and authors shall have neither liability nor responsibility to any person or entity with respect to any loss or damage caused, directly or indirectly, by the information contained in this book. If you do not wish to be bound by the above, you may return the book for a full refund.

About gender usage: In order to avoid numerous grammatical messes and to make the reading flow better, we have chosen to make this book as gender neutral as possible. We have used *they* and *their,* even for one person, instead of *he or she, his and hers,* and so on.

About the term *Realtor®*: This is a registered trademark of the National Association of REALTORS® (NAR), and anyone who uses that term as part of their professional identity must be a member not only of the NAR, but also of their local and state associations. We always encourage both buyers and sellers to seek out the services of a Realtor® when possible. However, even though we recommend the use of a Realtor®, we know there are many small communities in the country where there are no Realtors®. Often throughout this book, we refer to "agent," "licensee," "real estate salesperson," "broker," and so forth. We do this because anyone who holds a real estate sales license must abide by laws, which we will cover in Chapter 2. These laws apply to *all* real estate agents in the United States, not just Realtors®. To make the text easier to read you will see the term *Realtor®* used showing the registration mark and lower case letters after the initial capital *R*. Please also see Chapter 2 for a more complete explanation of this designation.

Again, please consult with a professional in your state based on your situation. You can also reach the authors directly through the contact information provided near the beginning and end of the book. Also, feel free to contact the authors for a referral to a Realtor® in your area.

Introduction by the Publisher

For many people, their home is the largest investment they will make in their lives. This book is designed to help you, as a homeowner, get the greatest return when you're ready to sell that asset. But right now your house is your home. It is the place where you shelter yourself from the outside world, where you raise children, bond with your mate, or express your individuality. When it comes time to sell your house (and your home) your thinking has to shift from a personal statement of who you are, or what your values are, to an investment vehicle that will appeal to the greatest audience. It needs to appeal to the specific demographics of your potential buyer. Remember, the prospective buyer will be comparing your house and home to all the others on the market that fit their needs, wants, and desires.

A small change or addition to your house can add thousands of dollars of profit to you, while spending money in the wrong way can actually cost you thousands more than you spent. You will see many examples in the following pages, but here is one example: If you spent $25,000 on a swimming pool, you would be lucky to get half of that back in the increased value of your home. In addition, you would pay additional property taxes, utility bills, and cleaning and maintenance costs over the life of the swimming pool.

Unfortunately, many people think they can save thousands of dollars by selling a home themselves. The requirements of disclosure when selling a home are getting as complicated as brain surgery. I guess someone in need of brain surgery could save thousands of dollars by reading medical manuals and then attempting to perform the operation themselves, but it would be silly. Just as silly is selling a home "by owner." How can the experience of selling one or even a few homes match the experience of a professional who does it day in and day out?

A study conducted by the National Association of REALTORS® determined that people who sold their homes themselves received 16 percent less than comparable homes where the owner used the services of a Realtor®. Another way of looking at this is to recognize that avoiding the services of an agent and saving about 7 percent—or less—on commissions cost 16 percent of the sales price that could have been received.

If you were a homebuyer you might be thinking that you're paying 16 percent more when you buy a home through a Realtor® instead of going direct to an owner. But based on national figures, the initial sale price an owner sets is well above the appropriate market price of comparable homes. In most situations a buyer working directly with a seller, with no agent support, will not know if the home is underpriced or overpriced. They won't know what inspector to hire to evaluate the integrity of the structure and systems, nor might they understand the responsibilities and liabilities of the other party. In many cases they will not know what forms and wording will provide the best protection if something goes wrong. And there are a host of other items that provide safeguards to both the buyer and the seller that they might not know. This book will cover all of these issues and more.

In this book, Wynne Achatz, Doug and Kathie Whitehouse, and Ken Deshaies expose the secrets of how Realtors® are able to get more money for home sellers and sell homes faster than those who attempt to do it for themselves. The authors not only share their own experiences, but have interviewed leading Realtors® from around the country in order to gather the best ideas and practices currently being used. If you are not already a homeowner but looking forward to buying your first home, this book can also give you invaluable insights into how to find the right home, finance the purchase, and save thousands of dollars in the process.

About the Authors

Wynne Achatz is an associate broker with Westrick Real Estate One involved with two offices—Algonac and Marine City, Michigan. She has many certifications demonstrating her educational background: Accredited Buyer Representative (ABR), Certified Residential Specialist (CRS), Internet Certified Professional (e-PRO), Referral and Relocation Coordinator (RRC), Performance Management Network (PMN) from the Woman's Council of REALTORS®, Leadership Training Graduate (LTG), Certified Real Estate Agents (CREA), REALTORS® Alumnae of Michigan (RAM), and the Graduate REALTORS® Institute (GRI) designation. In December of 2001, Wynne was one of the first 40 real estate agents in Michigan to receive the Senior Housing Real Estate Specialist (SHRES) designation. She is a member of the National Association of REALTORS® (NAR), the Real Estate Educators Association (REAA), and the Real Estate CyberSpace™ Society (RESC).

She has over 28 years of experience in the real estate business and is a lifelong resident of the area. Wynne is the fourth generation in a family business that began in Marine City in 1889. Wynne is truly a committed *real estate consultant.* "It's the personal service and attention that keep customers and clients coming back," she says. She knows that caring and giving back to her community and profession is what a true *real estate professional* practices. Wynne was the first to receive the "Perfect Partner" Award in the Real Estate One family of brokers statewide (Note: Real Estate One is Michigan's largest real estate company according to *Crain's Business Report*).

Wynne has been leading others in the use of technology in their business since 1996 when she became an Allen F. Hainge Seminar CyberStar™ and a CyberProfessional™. She has served her profession locally, statewide, and nationally on all association committees and in many offices. She currently chairs the state grievance committee. Wynne is a state licensed real estate educator and recommends attending all the state and national meetings.

In addition to being a full service agent, Wynne works closely with the finest mortgage companies, banks, title companies, and other professionals in the area to help make your real estate purchase or sale easy and trouble-free. She has written articles for *Realty Times, RIS Media, Real Estate Business Magazine,* and coauthored a book about the real estate transaction and buyer agency duties: *How To Make Your REALTOR® Get You The Best Deal,* Michigan Edition.

In 1999 and 2000, Wynne was president of the Marine City Chamber of Commerce. She brings technology adventures to Marine City, as well as energy and ideas for future growth and development of the area while preserving its historic integrity.

Her awards and achievements include: Real Estate One Master Marketing Award, High Volume Production Award for Franchise, Woman Realtor® of the Year 1992 and 1994, Realtor® of the Year 1993, and Michigan's Women's Council State Member of the Year 1999.

Her memberships and affiliations include: National Association of REALTORS®, Michigan Association of REALTORS®, Saint Clair County and Macomb County Association of REALTORS®, Several MLS systems, Marine City Rotary Club, Marine City and Anchor Bay Chamber of Commerce Member, and Internet Certification Association.

Wynne is a past MLS president and Saint Clair County Board of REALTORS® president, as well as a past state president of the Women's Council of REALTORS®. She has served on the Michigan Association State Board of Directors for four years, and has sat on the Public Policy Coordinating Committee since 1988.

To reach Wynne Achatz
(586) 260-7653
www.wynnea.com
sold@westrickteam.com
or
see page 139

Doug and Kathie Whitehouse are Realtors® in Michigan. Doug is the 2005 president of the Michigan Association of REALTORS® and Kathie is the 2005 Woman of the Year for the State of Michigan's Women's Council of REALTORS®. They hold the Realtor® Alumni of the University of Michigan (RAM), Accredited Buyer Representative (ABR), Certified Residential Specialist (CRS), Certified Internet Real Estate Professional (e-PRO), and Certified Residential Broker (CRB) designations. The Whitehouses are Allen F. Hainge CyberStars™—an elite group of Realtors® who have been nationally recognized as experts in using technology to successfully market real estate. Kathie was Women's Council of REALTORS® Chapter Member of the Year 2006 and Doug was recognized as Realtor® of the Year by his local association in 1994–1995. He has served as a director of several local associations as well as chairman of the board of the Regional Multiple Listing Service.

Doug works together as a team with his wife, Kathie, as a part of Hannett, Wilson & Whitehouse LLC, Realtors®, which services the Southeast Michigan area around Detroit. They specialize in Oakland, Macomb, and Wayne counties, as well as the lakes area. Oakland county, located just minutes north of Detroit, features loads of great lakefront homes and, with all of the major automobile manufacturers headquartered locally, it is considered one of the most upscale locations in the country to live in. Marketing homes of high quality requires the use of the latest in technology and exceptional creative skills to communicate the quality of lifestyle afforded by homes in the surrounding area.

Before becoming Realtors®, Doug and Kathie were part of a food processing company known as Whitehouse Products, which built the nondairy industry by creating the first commercially available nondairy whipped topping made from soybeans. During their leisure time they enjoy boating on all of the Great Lakes, from Chicago to the Canadian North Channel to Put-In-Bay in Lake Erie. If not on their boat you might see them on a Harley, enjoying a ride with either of their children on their own motorcycles.

To reach Doug and Kathie Whitehouse
(800) 210-9777
doug@whitehouses.com
www.whitehouses.com
or
see page 139

Ken Deshaies is a real estate broker in Colorado. He is an Accredited Buyer Representative (ABR), Certified Residential Specialist (CRS), Graduate of the REALTOR® Institute (GRI), one of the first 500 Realtors® in the country to become a Certified Internet Real Estate Professional (e-PRO500), Real Estate Cyberspace Specialist (RECS®), Allen F. Hainge CyberStar™ (an elite group of Realtors® who have proven that they generate a significant portion of their business through the use of current technology), and is EcoBroker™ certified. He has coauthored over 70 books on real estate. He was named CyberStar™ of the Year for 2002, and elected president of the Summit Association of REALTORS ® for 2003. He served on the committee for the Colorado Association of REALTORS® that spearheaded the change in agency laws effective in 2003. Ken serves on the Grievance Committee of the Colorado Association of REALTORS® and is an iSucceed mentor.

Ken works in partnership with his wife Mary in their brokerage, SnowHome Properties. He began his real estate career in Denver in 1992 and has worked in Summit County since 1994. Located an hour west of Denver, Summit County is home to four ski resorts and the highest freshwater sailing lake in the United States. While selling resort real estate is similar in many ways to selling in a metropolitan area, it offers unique problems. For example, since two out of three buyers are buying nonresidential properties, marketed materials, use of the Internet, and extensive use of digital photography are essential to a successful marketing plan.

Prior to real estate, Ken owned a private investigations firm for 12 years in Denver, employing and supervising as many as seven investigators, and serving for a period as the president of the Professional Private Investigators Association of Colorado. In this work, he conducted numerous investigations into real estate transactions and fraud claims. Many of the stories in this book are based on Ken's experiences, both before and after he became a Realtor®. During much of this time, he was also a member of the Win/Win Business Forum of Denver and was its president for a year and a half.

To reach Ken Deshaies
ken@snowhome.com
or see page 139

Selling Your Home: The Basics

1. Going It Alone

I wanted to take this opportunity to thank you for selling my home. I didn't realize there was such a difference among Realtors®. The quality of service you provided was courteous, professional, and encouraging. It far exceeded any previous experience I had. I believe you do work to become a client's Realtor® for life. It was a real pleasure. Should I need the services of a Realtor® in the future, you will be my first choice and I'm sure my last.

—Natalie Tyler

Many people who are considering selling their home are not sure how to begin this process. Do you try to sell your house on your own, or do you first enlist an agent? And if you want to try to sell your house on your own, will word get out there to that perfect buyer? The bottom line is that no matter which route you take to sell your home, you need to educate yourself as much as possible. In this area, where the economic stakes can be high, knowledge is power. By reading about the following experience, you will see what can sometimes happen in the sale of a home and understand why it pays to become educated. The following story is true and may possibly help you decide on whether or not selling your house on your own is a worthwhile measure to save money.

The Money to Move

A few years ago, Ken was searching for the right home for one of his buyers. He found a home not listed in his Multiple Listing Service (the local Realtor® database in which all available properties for sale are listed) that was being sold by the owner (called an FSBO in Realtor® parlance). It appeared that the home might fit his buyer's criteria, so he called the number listed on the flyer that the owner had posted in his yard.

Most FSBOs understand that even though they want to save the listing commission, in almost 95 percent of the cases it will be a Realtor® who brings in the buyer. Therefore, if they pay the Realtor® representing the buyer even something over half of a typical listing commission, they feel they are still saving money by not having to pay commission to a listing agent as well. That was the case here, when the owner, John, invited Ken to preview his home for a buyer. Ken visited with him and his wife later that day.

The home was in a family neighborhood, well maintained, and backed up to wetlands—all things that would add value to the selling price as compared to other homes on the market. However, John and Lucille were planning a move to another town and had calculated into their asking price what they felt they would need to facilitate their move and the purchase of another home in their new location. While they did have some knowledge of other home sales in the neighborhood, their calculations led them to establish an asking price roughly 15 percent over those comparable sales. They were asking $322,000 for a home that would have been properly priced to sell at about $290,000. When Ken met with them he was prepared with a market analysis and tried to explain that the differential they were seeking was more than the market would bear. They encouraged him to bring them an offer but made it clear they would stick fairly close to their asking price.

Ken's buyers did look at the home but declined to make an offer. Most buyers will offer less than an asking price, but very few will offer when they feel there is too much difference between asking price and market value.

Ken watched as John's ads reflected a price reduction to $312,000, but nearly three months later he finally listed with a Realtor® at full commission. Unfortunately, now the asking price was back at $322,000 since the sellers were hoping to recover part of the Realtor® commission in the sale price. After three months of attempts to sell, the price had dropped twice, eventually to $302,000. It was clear the sellers were getting anxious to move. Then Ken showed the home to another buyer who liked it and made an offer. However, his clients were first-time homebuyers with little cash and they needed a little assistance to get into the property. The offer was for $295,000 and asked the sellers to carry a small note of $10,000 for five years. In other words, the sellers were asked to lend the buyers part of the down payment. The buyers were creditworthy and otherwise fully capable of completing the purchase. However, Ken could not get the listing Realtor® to understand the simplicity of the financing and while the sellers would have taken the price, they declined the offer.

The home ultimately sold a couple of months later for $272,000. That was $50,000 less than their initial asking price, $23,000 less than Ken's buyer's offering price (the note would have been an extra bonus as it turned out), and around $18,000 to $25,000 less than the home would reasonably have sold for had it been properly listed from the start. We cannot tell you how many times we have seen this very scenario across the country. Homes sell for less than market because they are priced too high and become "stale." Homes that are on the market for much longer than normal market conditions indicate, often become the target of predatory buyers who understand that the seller is now more desperate and, hence, willing to cut their price.

Should I Try It Alone?

Although this story is not a guaranteed representation of the realities of selling your own home, what it does illustrate is that you must be educated. And often it pays to rely on an expert's education and experience.

If you do decide that you are prepared for the task of selling your own home, here are some important suggestions:

1. Take the time to educate yourself about the process of real estate transactions. Know how the process works from beginning to end, and what contractual and legal obligations you will be responsible for.

2. Know what transactions must be performed by outside professionals, such as inspectors, title agents, or attorneys.

3. Pay to have your house professionally appraised so that you price it correctly.

4. Have your home professionally inspected in advance, so that you know what might need to be repaired. Take care of those items you can afford to repair in advance.

5. Establish a marketing budget and determine the best ways to spend it.

6. Look for a preapproved, rather than a prequalified, buyer. There will be more on this distinction in the chapter regarding financing.

7. As a personal safety measure, *never* show your house alone.

8. Finally, understand that while it is your intention to save the real estate commission in the transaction, most buyers also understand

that and want the savings reflected in the purchase price.

Selling your house is not impossible, but it takes diligence, patience, diplomacy, and a willingness to set aside your own biases about your home so that other people's preferences can be understood and accommodated.

Knowing the Process

Before you decide to sell your own home, ask yourself these essential questions to ensure that you are knowledgeable about these important aspects of real estate sales:

- Do I know how to properly value my home?
- Do I have a marketing strategy to reach the greatest number of potential buyers?
- Am I familiar with Southeast Michigan's legal requirements for purchase contracts and real estate transfers?
- Can I ensure that the buyer is financially able to purchase my home?
- Do I have the necessary contracts to handle the closing transactions?
- Will my homeowner's insurance cover me for liability if a stranger to whom I am showing my home causes damage (to my home, my belongings, or me) or steals from me? (Recent stories involve people who steal prescription drugs from homes.)
- How are my negotiating skills?

- Am I prepared to carry back a note if an otherwise qualified buyer does not have the necessary down payment?
- Am I prepared to give up a partial commission to an agent representing a buyer or a full commission to a transaction broker (known in some states as a *facilitator*)?

The bottom line is that you must make sure you are prepared to deal with this major transaction. You should have a plan in place and you should know who can help you with aspects that you can't do alone. Just as money doesn't grow on trees, houses don't sell on their own. If you are selling your house yourself, you must be prepared to make a substantial investment of time. If you are not sure how to handle this complicated sales transaction, using a professional may save you a great deal of unnecessary complications.

2. Using a Real Estate Agent

Wynne was knowledgeable, open, honest, trustworthy, and comforting through the stress of it all.

—James Farrell and Cheryl Baitinger

A real estate agent and a Realtor® are not the same thing. Both may be experienced in the industry, but a Realtor® is a member of the National Association of REALTORS® and follows a specific code of ethics. We include more information on this in the following section, "Credentials." Anyone who passes their state's real estate licensing exam can become an agent. They may also be referred to as a *licensee* or *real estate salesperson* in other parts of the book. There are no cost differences between hiring an agent and a Realtor®.

Although there are some costs (you will pay a commission) associated with enlisting an agent or Realtor®, there are also substantial benefits. For instance, not only does a Realtor® have access to thousands of potential buyers that a homeowner may not be aware of, they also have the knowledge to make sure that you are protected both financially and legally. Additionally, there is some element of risk involved in selling your home besides the obvious economic risk. Realtors® know important legal disclosure requirements. Agents are well aware of the fact that you are allowing complete strangers into your home; therefore, they know what precautions you should take to protect both your family and your possessions.

One of the most important advantages of listing with a Realtor® is their access to the Multiple Listing Service (MLS). This is a proprietary database of almost all the local property listings. The MLS was designed by Realtors® to share listing information with other Realtor® members. The MLS provides the greatest exposure for your property listing, which increases your chances of a quicker sale at a better price. Approximately 98 percent of all properties are sold by MLS members.

But these are just a few of the reasons why enlisting the help of a Realtor® is a good investment. A Realtor® can do the following:

- use extensive data and professional experience to determine the best selling price for your home;
- provide information about your home to thousands of potential buyers and their agents;
- screen buyers and negotiate a sales contract;
- take on potential legal obligations and risks; and
- take you through every step of the process, all the way to closing.

What to Look For

Credentials

Picking an agent is a business decision that should be taken with the same deliberation as any other important financial decision. You want an agent who specializes in your market area, who is experienced, and who you are confident will work hard for you. You've probably noticed that when we've used the term *Realtor®* in this book, it is capitalized and the registration mark is used. There is a reason for that. The term *Realtor®* is a trademark of the National Association of REALTORS® (NAR), and anyone who uses that term as part of their professional identity must be a member, not only of NAR but of their state and local associations. Anyone who is not a member, but is legitimately working in the real estate profession, is still licensed by their state real estate commission and can be identified as an agent, a real estate salesperson, a real estate broker, and so on.

When *Realtor®* is used, however, it means several things. NAR members have training available only to members. They have the benefit of local meetings and state and national conferences where they can network with other Realtors®. Many deals are actually made for buyers and sellers at those events.

There is a price to pay: NAR members subscribe to a code of ethics, which commits them to conduct their business with a sense of fair play. The public has some recourse when they feel they have been lied to, mistreated, or cheated. They can file an ethics complaint with the local association requesting that a Realtor® be disciplined, or request arbitration if they feel they have actually been cheated out of money. The Grievance Committee and the Professional Standards Committee of the organization handle these complaints. While a member is not bound to submit to the grievance process when a complaint is initiated by buyers or sellers, most do so because it is a much simpler and less costly method of justice than going to court.

Members have to pay dues, and the MLS charges other fees to maintain a membership in good standing, but the bottom line is that they are in a position to provide much better service to you than nonmembers.

Those who do not have the Realtor® designation are operating independently. They often do not do enough business to justify the costs involved in belonging to the NAR. They are not bound by a code of ethics that governs their professional actions, and in some areas they do not have the benefit of MLS access.

So for starters, get a Realtor®. You'll usually find the designation on their business card.

History

If you were taking in a roommate or boarder, you would screen that person to see if you were compatible. If you were renting out property, you would take a rental application and check out the renter's references and credit history. If you were going into business with someone, you would be smart to conduct a background check. It never hurts to know who you are working with. The same is true with a real estate agent.

As consumers, we have a terrible history of picking professionals—doctors, lawyers and, yes, real estate agents. We get a referral from a friend, attend the appointment, and that's usually as far as we go. If we end up dissatisfied later, it's our own fault for not taking responsibility for our own selection. We need to prescreen, ask questions, get a feel for how compatible we might be, and determine how well that professional can meet our needs.

If you have a friend in the business, it can be difficult to select someone else, but it might be the most valuable decision you can make. We have known people who listed their homes with a friend who specialized in commercial sales but had never sold a house. You need to ask some questions before starting with any real estate agent. Don't sit down and say, "We're looking for a house in the $400,000 range." Try something like, "Before we start, I'd like to learn a few things about you." Interview your potential agent, ask questions, and determine the following important issues to your satisfaction.

Questions to ask a potential agent:

- What other type of work do you do?

- Do you work full-time in real estate?

- How flexible is your schedule?

- How available are you to show properties on weekdays, weekends, mornings, and evenings?

Get a Full-Time Agent or a Professional Team

Most full-time agents work 50 to 60 hours a week or more. They are committed to their work and to their clients. A part-time agent is there to make a deal when it comes along, but either doesn't need the income a full-time career produces or isn't making it yet, and may hold two or more jobs. Within reasonable limits, a Realtor® should fit their schedule to yours, not the other way around, and should be available and easy to get in contact with regardless of their hours. On the other hand, agents who have spent some years building their business will often enlist assistants or team members. Doug and his wife, Kathie, along with an administrative staff, make up the Whitehouse team. They may then be in a position to take more time off, but have qualified team members to show property and oversee the details of transactions. Team leaders train their team members in their system, and in the quality of customer service that the leader has developed over the years. Teams usually have specialists handling different parts of the transaction, so you will almost always have someone available to provide seamless service. This can be especially beneficial if your Realtor® is on vacation or busy attending to other clients' needs. Wynne works basically on her own and will refer buyers to other agents. When the occasion arises and she is called out of town, she shares commissions with the agent who covers for her.

Get an Agent Who Is Busy

Ask your potential agent how many sides they closed last year and the year before. A "side" is one side of the sale. When one Realtor® has the property listing and another one brings in the buyer, each produces one "side" when the transaction closes. An agent who has closed only four to eight sides in a year is not doing enough business to merit having yours. They probably need money, just got started, can't get enough business to survive, or are on their way into another profession. An agent who has done 15 or 20 sides is not making a great deal of money but is surviving and probably growing, and, believe it or not, they're far above the national average.

An agent who is doing 30 or more sides a year is very busy—usually for a reason. They have attracted business, hopefully because they have served people well, although some Realtors® generate lots of business simply through smart advertising. It is, therefore, important to get a sense of how many transactions were results of referrals from past clients.

Questions to ask an agent:

- How many sides did you close last year?
- Is that usual for you?
- How many sides did you close the year before?

Now that you know how busy the agent is, ask how many of those sides were working with sellers and how many were representing buyers.

- What percent of your business comes from representing sellers?
- How much of your business comes from referrals?

Check Out the Broker's Specialty

If you are selling a home, select an agent who specializes in residential sales. If you want to buy an apartment building or a business, select someone who specializes in commercial sales. There are numerous specialties in real estate, and your agent's specialty should be consistent with your goals. In larger metropolitan areas, Realtors® also tend to specialize in geographic areas, in price ranges or with types of buyers. An agent who primarily sells million-dollar homes won't have the time for a $100,000 home.

Questions to ask an agent:

- Do you have a specialty?
- What are the price ranges of the homes you sell?
- What area/region do you specialize in?
- Do you sell commercial and residential real estate?

Make Sure the Broker Is Technologically Current

In today's world, it is vitally important to work with professionals who are computer literate and have a grasp on the new gadgets designed to improve service to their customers.

Many states require Realtors® to use certain forms in real estate transactions. These forms are almost always available on computer programs, which provide the quickest, most accurate way to generate contracts. Those who continue to write their contracts by hand or use a typewriter to fill in the blanks on standard forms are living in the past, demonstrating an unwillingness to keep up with the times and may not be capable of providing the best service.

Wynne and Doug receive 92–98 percent of all their leads from the Internet. They both feel that their Internet presence and website style are critical to their business. Doug keeps connected with his Blackberry wireless PDA/phone and his tablet computer. They both find most marketing or advertising money is going to the Internet and away from hard copy (newspapers, magazines, and so forth).

Other types of software allow Realtors® to track their customer's needs, access increasingly more sophisticated MLS systems, and communicate by email. Digital cameras allow photos and virtual tours of your home, complete with interior and exterior views.

If the real estate agent you are interviewing is not able to utilize a computer, beat a hasty retreat. Your house should have as much Internet exposure as possible. Your wonderful home could be passed over while a competing house that is visible on the Internet is quickly snatched up.

Questions to ask your agent:

- Can I have your email address?

- What is the address of your website? Do you have more than one? What others do you link to? What sites link to yours?

- Will you take digital pictures of my home? How many will appear in the MLS and in other marketing materials? Will you create a virtual tour of my home?

- Do you also do print advertising?

- Can you show me samples of your listings, flyers, ads, and websites?

- What are the ways in which you generate leads and how do those ways relate to each other? In other words, what is your marketing plan?

- What forms do you typically download for use?

- What other technology do you use in your business?

Training

Anyone worth their salt in any profession continues to update their knowledge about the work they do. Doctors, lawyers, and mechanics face an ever-changing world when it comes to their professions and must take classes to continue to be of service to their customers. The same is true of Realtors®.

Michigan's state law requires continuing education, but the requirements are minimal: 18 hours every three years for everyone with a license. Good Realtors® find the time to take much more training than that. There are a number of designations denoting certain continuing education landmarks and they are often signified on business cards in the form of letters following their name. While some may be in areas not related to residential sales, all show a commitment on behalf of the Realtor® to keep their professional skills honed, and that's good. Do not work with someone who demonstrates no interest in continuing education. Look for some of the following designations on your prospective agent's business card:

GRI—Graduate REALTORS® Institute—represents approximately 80 hours of advanced education beyond the training that is required to be licensed. It is usually the first step to becoming more informed and professional.

CRS—Certified Residential Specialist—requires completion of numerous two- to three-day classes held around the country. It takes the average Realtor® a few years to complete and usually costs $5,000 to $10,000 in tuition and travel costs. It provides significantly increased and detailed knowledge in residential issues and is the "graduate degree" of residential sales. Graduates are members of the Residential Sales Council (RSC) and receive continuing information in a variety of ways to keep them abreast of new issues in the area.

ALC—Accredited Land Counselor—similar to the CRS, this usually requires several years and several thousand dollars to achieve. It's the "graduate degree" of land sales.

CCIM—Certified Commercial Investment Member—this designates experts in commercial property sales, like shopping centers and industrial, office, and apartment buildings. It requires extensive continuing education and graduates are members of the Commercial Sales Council.

e-PRO—Certified Internet Real Estate Professional—This is the only certification program of its kind recognized nationwide and endorsed by the National Association of REALTORS®. Those searching for a Realtor® can have confidence that e-PRO graduates are savvy with all aspects of the Internet. They not only take the Internet-empowered consumer seriously, they are also able to meet their online needs.

CyberStar™—An Allen F. Hainge CyberStar™ is one of an elite group of Realtors® from around the country and abroad who have proven efficiency in the use of technology and have agreed to serve as teaching professionals with Allen. They work well with people on the Internet, with email, and in person. They are top producers in their markets, and even have exclusive territories. Their websites are often the most innovative and provide the most local information.

Attitude

We cannot just end this section without a discussion about attitude and disposition. A good, winning attitude means a lot—we would much rather work with a newly licensed agent who really wants to help than some old curmudgeon who has been in the profession for years, thinks they have all the answers, and won't listen to anything new. There are a lot of worn-out real estate agents who have "seen it all" still occupying desk space in offices across the land.

Your initial interview with a prospective agent will tell you a lot about their approach to life. Work with an optimist, not a pessimist. Listen to their answers to your questions. You do not want one who says, "Your house is going to be hard to sell," but rather, "It might be difficult to find the right buyer, but I know that the right exposure can get your house sold."

It isn't brain surgery to figure this out; look for a good, positive attitude as part of your evaluation process.

Summary of Recommended Qualifications

Your success in selling your home is dependent on the quality of the agent you select to represent you in that sale. You know that an agent doesn't get paid until a sale occurs. So, would you be concerned if an agent were unable or afraid to spend the necessary money to properly expose your home to potential buyers? Would you be concerned if an agent simply put your property listing into a multiple listing service (MLS), put up a sign, and prayed that it would sell?

In Summit County, Ken has over 600 Realtor® members in his association. But 90 percent of the real estate transactions are facilitated by only about 10 percent of the agents. Around half of his agents sell one or zero properties a year. Of course, many are intentionally part-time. The membership turns over 25 percent each year. You would be well advised to determine where your agent ranks. This is an important decision. So, choose an agent using our following recommendations:

- They know how to get your home the best exposure. More exposure increases the chances of your home selling for the best price.

- They have a personal website and that site is content-rich and places well in the Internet search engines. In 2005, 80 percent of all homebuyers in the United States started on the Internet. Often, they selected their agent prior to shopping for their home.

- They advertise in print publications. Though not the best way to obtain buyers, repetition of the company name will create more traffic for all.

- They spend an appropriate amount of money on other advertising.

- They produce a virtual tour or slide show of your property and place it on the Internet for buyers to see. Two-thirds of buyers who viewed properties on the Internet indicated that they look for virtual tours, and all website visitors want to see lots of photos.

- Your Realtor® knows how to use a camera and uses it frequently. Too many agents take only one photo of a property and some take none at all. Digital cameras make taking photos easy and inexpensive. There is no reason that you should not have the maximum number of photos allowed in your MLS listing and many more on agent and other websites. The only exception might be if you were selling a distressed property that just did not photograph well at all.

- They believe in continuing education to keep up on the latest in selling techniques and networking with agents locally and in other locales. Most successful agents attend conferences around the country where they meet other agents, and they then refer business to each other.

- They always follow through. Would it be important to you to get feedback from your agent along the course of the time your house is on the market? Successful agents have mechanisms in place to obtain feedback from other agents who show your property and pass that information to you. They will also keep you abreast of other matters that might affect your property, its condition, pricing, and so on.

- They cover their market. If a successful agent works well in the entire geographic market serviced by the local MLS, it is better to work with that agent than one who is less successful, but closer to your home.

While no one can guarantee a quick sale, an agent who performs with the above qualifications will make your selling experience smoother, will cause you less anxiety, and will provide the highest possibility for a successful sale.

Agency Liability

It is important to discuss the concept of agency, so that you can understand how representation works. It's easy to use words like *sub-agency* and *real estate agency*, but the fact of the matter is that *agency* is a legal term. Its use confers a legal obligation and some legal liability.

Let's say, for example, that your parents are going to be away on a vacation for an extended period of time. While they are gone, they want someone to deposit their checks, pay their bills, and carry on business for them as usual. What they want, in fact, is someone to keep their best interests in mind and to act accordingly. They ask you to represent them and to handle the paperwork for them in their absence. In order for you to legally perform those functions, they would have to sign a document giving you power to act on their behalf. This document is called a *power of attorney,* and it makes you their *agent,* or legal representative.

The basic principal is that an agent is often in a better position to handle their client's business than is the client. The agent is either physically in a better location to handle business for the client or is more knowledgeable about the matters to be handled. You hire an attorney and the attorney becomes your agent, because the attorney understands law and you do not. Similarly, you hire a real estate agent to sell your home because the agent is in the best position to represent you in the sale of your home.

There is, however, one other aspect of agency that merits discussion: *vicarious liability.* Most people understand that a liability is a risk; it's an exposure. You take on a liability when you hire an attorney to take actions on your behalf. If that attorney signs a contract on your behalf that creates an unattractive obligation to a third party, you are still liable for your attorney's actions. Your child could damage the property of another, and you might be held responsible for reparations. That is vicarious liability. It extends your risk through reliance on, or responsibility for, others.

Every time you engage an agent to represent you, you take on some vicarious liability. You rely on your agent to make decisions and recommendations that are in your best interest. You have also engaged that agent because you believe their knowledge in the area is greater than yours and, you hope, greater than others in the same field. Therefore, when retaining a Realtor® be aware that you may take on some vicarious liability. It will behoove you to ensure that your agent is experienced, knowledgeable, professional, and willing and able to work for you. In the following sections, we present the basic descriptions of agency.

Single Agency

With the changes in the laws governing real estate, many states created a term, called *single agency*. Under *single agency*, a seller could be represented by one real estate salesperson (*agent*), and a buyer could be represented by another real estate salesperson (*agent*). Some balance was potentially brought to the transaction. We say potentially, because many real estate salespeople around the country had to learn new rules. Some agents made the transition easily and happily and some did not. There was, and still is, some resistance in the real estate community to buyer's agents, but it is diminishing over time. Transactions are becoming less adversarial, and both buyers and sellers are feeling more fairness in the deals they make.

By far the most important aspect of these new laws is how they fleshed out and defined the single agency relationship. Generally, they established some procedures and indicators by which one could tell if the relationship was there. Single agency is a procedure whereby a single agent can represent a buyer and another single agent can represent a seller, each with their own obligations. Single agents are to:

- exercise reasonable skill and care on behalf of their seller or buyer;

- promote the client's interests with the utmost good faith, loyalty, and fidelity;

- if they are a seller's agent, instruct the seller to disclose any known adverse material defects of the property;

- counsel the client as to those benefits and risks of the transaction actually known to the broker;

- advise the client to seek expert assistance where needed;
- account in a timely manner for money and property; and
- inform the client of the exposure to vicarious liability for the acts and omissions of agents working on the client's behalf.

Single agency laws require buyers and sellers to be informed consumers. It remains to be seen how well it works in practice.

Dual Agency

This is not a new term, but its use poses a hurdle many feel is impossible to overcome. Dual agency can exist whenever the same real estate firm represents both the buyer and seller in the same transaction. It requires the broker to simultaneously be an agent and an advocate for both the buyer and seller in the same transaction. This can obviously create conflicting allegiances. When an agent with one realty company represents a seller and an agent with another company represents a buyer, there is little conflict. When you sign a contract, you are retaining the agent's entire company to represent you in your purchase or sale.

The dual agent has the responsibility not to disclose to either party without the prior consent of the other the following issues: (1) whether the buyer may pay more or the seller may take less; (2) the motivating factors for either party; (3) whether the buyer or seller would agree to different financial terms; (4) any facts or suspicions about circumstances that potentially represent a psychological stigma on the property; and (5) any material information about the other party, unless nondisclosure would constitute fraud or dishonest dealing.

There Are Advantages to Dual Agency

As much as we feel dual agency is harmful to consumers, it does have some advantages. If you are dealing with only one firm, and especially if there is only one individual agent involved, your lines of communication are shorter. For example, if you ask your agent a question that requires input from the other party, you are likely to get a faster answer since there is one less firm in the chain of communication.

Another advantage may be one of motivation. If one firm is earning both sides of the commission, they are more motivated to do what they can to make the transaction close if a major obstacle surfaces. This is to your benefit, unless the obstacle was your desire to cancel the transaction.

To protect yourself, discuss the firm's agency policy in your initial contact with them. Ask them to explain how they prevent dual agency from occurring. Of course, the agent you choose will also have to be experienced and competent in the rest of the skills needed to serve you.

Non-Agency

Some states have embraced an alternative to dual agency: *non-agency*. In a non-agency relationship, the firm has no fiduciary responsibilities to anyone. This arrangement is not attractive to consumers for the obvious reason: there are very few circumstances in which you would hire a firm that has no responsibility to you, and possibly no liability if they damage you.

Transaction Brokerage

Some states have adopted a completely new concept called transaction brokerage. It provides a radical and sometimes workable method of handling inhouse transactions. Generally, it is described as a broker who assists one or more parties throughout a contemplated real estate transaction with communication, advisement, contract terms, and the closing of such transaction without being an agent or advocate for the interests of either party.

Transaction brokerage requires both parties to step back from the agency relationship to neutrality. The arrangement can make an inhouse transaction work. Your agent can show your property to buyers who fit your needs, desires, and financial abilities. If an inhouse listing fits a buyer, it should be shown to them. If they want to purchase your property, your agent lets them determine how to construct the offer and simply carries it back and forth between the seller and buyer until the two of you reach an agreement. The same neutral attitude is carried through each step of the process until the sale is closed.

Commissions

In this country, commissions have historically been paid out of the proceeds of the sale, so it has been presumed that the seller actually pays those commissions; however, this is not entirely true. Some professionals believe that because it is the buyer who actually brings the money to the transaction, the buyer pays the commission.

Additionally, new agency laws have started to change this tradition by stating that any party to a transaction may pay any broker's compensation without creating or terminating any agency relationship within that transaction. And more importantly, home values are established in this country with real estate commissions factored in as part of the value. That is because home sales have been, and almost always are, handled by real estate agents. The cost of that handling becomes part of the ultimate sale price and value of the home. Therefore, it becomes a moot point who pays the commission—it is simply part of the home value and paid out of the proceeds of the sale. Please be aware that listing commission amounts or percentages are negotiable, and the form of commission agreed upon may vary as well. There is no "standard" or "normal" commission.

One thing to be aware of is that agents are not allowed to charge you any fee on top of their commission unless it is explicitly stated in the contract. It is always important to know your rights before you enlist any personal representative.

The bottom line is that you should not let the dollar amount of a Realtor's® commission scare you away. It can be an invaluable investment. Just as in many complex transactions, expertise costs money but it is usually well worth the price.

How Much Goes to Your Agent?

If you feel the listing agent actually gets to keep the entire listing commission, you haven't asked enough questions. While it is not always the case, it is typical that the listing agent offers half their listing commission to an agent working with a buyer who brings in a successful contract. Each of those agents then has to split their portion of the commission with their broker. The broker usually incurs the cost of keeping an office open, staffed, and equipped. The broker's portion of the listing agent's split is meant to pay for that overhead and, hopefully, provide some profit. If your agent is the broker, then they are incurring those costs themselves.

Studies have shown that the cost of being in business in real estate can amount to much more than 50 percent of earnings. Now, obviously, a broker whose agents sell less will have a higher percentage of earnings going to overhead, and one who sells more can expect less overhead and more profit. It is not unusual for half the agent's split to go to the broker. Many times, that split is structured more in favor of the agent as the agent's production goes up. But, you can easily see that your listing agent may only be keeping one-quarter of the listing commission that you are paying, and your agent has additional expenses of their own. Brokers do not cover all costs. Agents generally have to provide their own vehicles for showing (and they cannot be old and run down), as well as their own cell phones. They also pay their own dues, insurance, continuing education, and at least part of their advertising costs.

How important is the sale of your home? Do you want it sold at the best price and in a timely manner? As with any professional service, you can search for the least expensive vendor or you can search for the most qualified. The most qualified will generally cost you more, but you can often measure the savings. At the very least, you get the additional peace of mind knowing your are in good hands.

The Discounters

We have taken many property listings after they have been on the market anywhere from three months to a year or so with a discount broker. What are discount brokers? Well, we believe they are often the ones who provide "discount services" and who don't spend much money or effort getting exposure for your property. But they are also the ones who *advertise* that they will charge you less than anyone else. There are often a couple of problems associated with such listings. Once the property has spent sufficient time on the market without a sale, even if it has been priced properly, it may have to come down in price in order to generate new interest in the property. There are currently companies that will take your property listing and not provide any service–with the exception of placing the property in the local MLS. Agents working with buyers are not offered a cooperative fee split, or if they are, it's a nominal fee that can be as low as $1.00. The agent is instructed to bring their buyer's offer direct to the seller and to negotiate directly. That buyer's agent then, in order to get paid for their work, must write a commission into the contract or will have to collect it directly from their buyer. And if that agent doubts their ability to get paid if they sell a property, what do you think the prospects of them actually showing it are?

This following point is made by our good friend and Realtor®, Mollie Wasserman, from her forthcoming book on real estate consulting:

> "MLS Entry Only" is one of the biggest travesties foisted on the public. Not only is it a legal liability (people think that if you are their agent, you're representing them, no matter what they sign), it doesn't work! That is the big reason I will not offer MLS Entry Only. Despite advertising claims to the contrary, we know from sales data over the last couple of years that MLS Entry Only is usually a waste of money for the vast majority of sellers. The MLS was designed as a co-operative between licensed agents, not an advertising medium for unrepresented sellers. When the MLS is used as intended, agents know that they will have a licensed partner on the other side who will not only provide the fiduciary counsel to their own client, but also complete the many tasks required of an agent. MLS Entry Only listings notoriously get far fewer showings because buyer agents know they will have to deal directly with the seller and often have to do the work for both sides. Because of this, and the lack of fiduciary counsel, many

> MLS Entry Only listings do not sell, forcing the seller to then hire a full service agent and forfeit their MLS Entry Only fee. If their home does sell, it usually receives thousands of dollars less than it should have for being a party to this consumer rip-off.

Now, consider if you were the buyer and had to pay your agent's commission on top of paying for the home. You could not include the commission in the financing, because it is not in the purchase price. So, it would be additional money out of pocket.

If financing were to be part of the deal, you would likely lose that buyer. And if you will be paying the buyer's agent directly (usually more than half a "normal" listing commission), you might as well engage a full service Realtor® from the beginning, eliminate the headaches, and have someone capable, willing, and obligated to provide you with good advice throughout the listing/sale process.

As of this writing, 10 states have passed legislation requiring licensed real estate agents to provide a set minimum amount of service, regardless of what they charge. A number of additional states are considering similar legislation. Part of the impetus has been complaints from homeowners who did not understand that they would have to do virtually everything in the transaction and pay the fees as well. The Department of Justice has indicated that it may take this to court on antitrust grounds, but the National Association of REALTORS® has said it will aggressively fight for the states and their consumers.

Bundled Service Companies

A relatively new type of brokerage that offers more payment choices are those entities called "bundled service" companies. These are companies that may provide the entire range of real estate service, but let you choose which you want. You may decide, for example, to hold your own open house and do your own advertising—and hence, pay a smaller fee. Ultimately, you get to decide full-service or less. Just be aware of the differences. Accepting less service may save you money, but it places added burden on you to create a sale.

3. The Role of the Internet

> Creative, forward thinking, and helpful. Wynne's use of email and technology made the transactions easier. Our Realtor® for life! Seven purchases and sales.
>
> —Robert, Jennifer, Alana, and Cooper Jannette

Given the revolution in technology that we've experienced over the last few years, we must look at *what technology can and cannot do*. This differentiation is especially crucial when dealing with real estate, an environment where online companies clutter the bandwidth and your inbox with schemes to save incredible amounts of money and time by using their services.

Now let's be clear: technology, and specifically the Internet, is a wonderful thing! Technology is a fabulous way to gather data and can do *functionary* tasks better, faster, and cheaper than any human being ever could. But the danger does not lie in understanding that technology. The danger is that by itself, the Internet can never provide the *fiduciary* counsel required in services such as mortgage lending, law, and real estate.

Functionary and *fiduciary*—why do we keep using these words? Simply, it's very important to understand the difference between the data that you can get online and the advice, counsel, and interpretation of that data that only your Realtor® can provide.

Information Versus Knowledge

As Internet-savvy Realtors® who generate a significant portion of our business online, we are big believers in the free flow of information. You will find that both online and off, this new breed of Realtor® usually provides the most complete sources of information that you'll find anywhere.

Yet, we have had many of our colleagues question why we give out so much information, often saying "If you give out too much information, people will have no reason to call you." We disagree. Although we give out information freely, we have never had a shortage of requests to retain our services. That's because there's a big difference between *information* and *knowledge*.

John Tuccillo states in his book, *The Eight New Rules of Real Estate*, "Information is a collection of facts or observations about reality. Knowledge is actionable." In today's information age, consumers can increasingly get all the information that they want or need, but it's useless unless someone with expertise in the field can provide the knowledge to allow them to correctly act on it. Information, without the context of a pro who can share the day-to-day knowledge of the industry, is just *data*. If a consumer were to act on it without context, they could very well reach incorrect conclusions and achieve undesirable results.

Information is like sand on a beach—it's plentiful and anyone can find it. But if you want to build a sandcastle, you may want to consult the sand master who lives on the beach. They can tell you how much water to use, what weather conditions are best for building, and, most importantly, when the tide comes in and how far up. Without this knowledge, you could spend an entire afternoon building a great sandcastle, only to have it washed away too soon!

Myths Involving Real Estate and the Internet

People definitely love to surf the Internet when it comes to real estate. It's estimated that last year, over 80 percent of homebuyers started their search online. But there are definitely myths about what the Internet can and cannot do. The following myth is one of our favorites:

"The Internet is great! I can...
1. buy a book
2. buy an airline ticket
3. buy or sell a house
4. get legal advice
5. receive a medical opinion

. . . *all* online!"

At what point did the above statement step over the line from fact to myth? If you say after number two, the airline ticket, give yourself a gold star! What's the difference between the first two products and the last three services? Simple. *The first two are commodities bought mostly by price, the last three are services that require counsel, advice, knowledge, and understanding of your individual needs.* The first two are functionary products, the last three are fiduciary services. You can purchase the first two products entirely online and probably save money in the process. In regards to the last three services, the Internet is a great place to start your search for service providers. But if you try to "go it alone" with just the data you find online, you will very likely risk losing your shirt if you don't consult a local provider who understands your individual needs and is accountable for their services.

Let's look at a couple of obvious examples before turning to real estate. Let's say there's an online site called WeKnowLaws-R-Us.com. For $39.95, payable in advance by credit card, you can receive a "legal opinion." Does this opinion come from an attorney, a paralegal, or a truck driver? The site *says* it's from an attorney, but how do you know for sure? And what if you take this legal advice and your case turns out badly? How do you get out of the deeper legal dilemma you're now in? Local attorneys who are dependent on referrals for future business have a great incentive to stand behind their advice and counsel. Does whoever at WeKnowLaws-R-Us out there in Dot-Com Land care if you're unhappy with their opinion? In other words, what happens if something goes wrong?

The Closing That Almost Didn't Happen

Recently, the SnowHome Team closed a transaction for a buyer client who had insisted on using an out-of-area lender. Now, of course, it is inappropriate for a Realtor® to "steer" a buyer to a particular lender, especially if the Realtor® is making a fee for doing so. However, it is normal for their agent to recommend a few mortgage brokers with whom they have experience. Typically, they will know brokers who are not only competitively priced, but who (1) have access to dozens of investors (the banks and mortgage companies who ultimately take the loan); (2) pay attention to detail; (3) communicate well with both the buyer and their agent (and when instructed, with the listing agent); and (4) are sufficiently organized to anticipate problems before they occur. When an unexpected problem crops up, they are capable of responding quickly to adjust the process—very often with successful results. But, when a buyer insists on using a lender of their choice, whether chosen from past experience or because of a cost break, the Realtor® is in a position of having to accept the buyer's choice.

The buyer, whom we will call Melinda, provided the contact information for her out-of-area lender, and in spite of Ken's recommendations, insisted that she wanted to use that lender. The first red flag was when it took several calls over several days to get a return call from her lender, whom we'll call Joe. Joe was doing an unusually aggressive loan for Melinda (100 percent financing with the seller paying closing costs), but insisted from the start that there would be no problem with the loan, that she was a "shoe-in." A second red flag was the difficulty in getting progress reports from Joe. He had over a month to process the loan, but was poor at returning calls or otherwise keeping us apprised of the progress. The appraisal was not ordered in time to meet a contract deadline, so the deadline had to be extended. Nevertheless, Joe insisted he would have the loan approved in time. Finally, just one day prior to the scheduled closing on the property, Joe called to say the sellers would have to extend the closing for a few days so that he could get final underwriting approval. The sellers had become frustrated by this time, and indicated they would prefer to cancel the contract (and Melinda would lose her earnest money) rather than extend again. And Melinda was also frustrated, but it was clearly too late to switch lenders. So, Joe, under duress, got the loan approved, sent his numbers to the title company at the last minute, and the transaction was closed.

Well, it wasn't actually closed because, in spite of the fact that both buyer and seller signed all the necessary documents, the funds did not arrive from the lender. This was on a Friday morning, and based on information from the lender that the funds would be wired shortly and should arrive by the end of the day, the seller agreed to let Melinda take possession of the property and move in. Over the weekend, Melinda spent around $2,000 getting the interior of the property painted, moving in, and purchasing accessories. Of course, the funds had not arrived on Friday, but everyone anticipated receipt on Monday.

During this entire process, we communicated regularly with the listing agent, and even put that agent in direct contact with Melinda's lender. The seller's agent was understandably concerned throughout, but his being "wired in" and understanding what was going on helped facilitate our efforts. Monday encompassed a flurry of activity when the funds did not show up with the normal wire, and the title company received word from the lender that the funds had been sent to the wrong company. The lender blamed the title company for providing the wrong wiring instructions, even though the title company used the same fax form with preprinted instructions that it had used for years. The seller was becoming increasingly frustrated, and finally said that if they were not in receipt of funds by 5:00 p.m., they would terminate the transaction, Melinda would have to move out, and she would also sacrifice her earnest money. Of course, she would also lose the time and money she spent to remodel the property. The gravity of this situation was conveyed to Joe, and it was made clear that Melinda had legal recourse to him and his company for any damages she might suffer as a result of his ineptitude. Well, the funds arrived just a little after 4:00 p.m., and the transaction was saved.

Melinda was not only apologetic to everyone, but she states that she will always use a recommended lender in the future. Had the rest of the team in place not been prepared for emergencies, this sale would clearly have been lost, and everyone in the transaction would have suffered.

As a seller, you simply need to be aware that (1) there are both good and bad lenders, (2) buyers have a choice of which company they might use, and (3) it often takes good Realtors® on both sides to insure that everything runs smoothly and that contingency plans are in place.

There is one other point. Agents who have experience on both sides of a transaction will usually have a better understanding of the other side and more of a proclivity to help when needed.

So, in addition to the lender who is in the neighborhood, or happens to be a friend or family member, there are also the online mortgage companies that advertise everywhere. If you've read the business section of the paper lately, you know that many of these companies are not doing so well. Why is this? Well, there are a couple of reasons. First, much of the mortgage process still has to be done locally, so there's little economy to doing the process online, and more importantly, many consumers are finally catching on that interest rates and financing programs are very vulnerable to the old bait and switch that we mentioned earlier. Do you really think for a moment that the online mortgage company in "Anywhereland" is particularly concerned if you're unhappy with their services? A local mortgage lender derives business from local Realtors® and the community. Therefore, they have to make the situation right because they must be *accountable*! The national dot-com may not feel that way. Now, as we said earlier, the Internet is a wonderful place to shop rates and programs and to educate yourself on the mortgage process. But afterwards, do yourself a favor and bring the best package to your Realtor's® recommended lender and ask if they can match it. Either they will, or they'll tell you why they can't.

Have you ever been to a medical website? There are many wonderful sites out there. If you were to go to one to become a more educated patient, and then take your questions and concerns to your doctor, that would be a very smart use of the Internet. If, however, you were to go to a site and attempt to diagnose yourself, that would be a very unintelligent use of information, with potentially disastrous results.

Real estate is an interesting field in that it combines functionary tasks with fiduciary counsel. Functionary tasks, such as property searches or accessing home sales data, can always be done cheaper, faster, and better by technology. If that was the whole of real estate, we'd be the first to applaud the national dot-coms popping up online promising to provide you these services without your having to leave the computer. But the problem is that these companies don't tell you what you *don't* get. As an example, there are a couple of companies that heavily advertise that you can get a *free* home valuation online. All you have to do is give them a street address and it's yours. So what *do* you get? (Drum roll please.) A list of homes sold within a one-mile radius of that address. Does this "home valuation," coming from a national site, take into account the power plant going in two blocks away from this home, which will affect its value? Has it seen the inside of the home to find out how it compares with others? Does it take into account the railroad tracks on the next street? What about the local economy and the fact that young professionals are moving into the area, accelerating the increase in prices? What about sewer abatements or the newest regulations? A national dot-com can't advise you of any of those things, which can greatly affect the value of the property, but a Realtor® who's working in your interest can.

Please remember that while the Internet can provide information, it cannot interpret it! A Realtor's® real value is not just in using technology to market your home but in bringing those buyers to you and helping you make the most money when selling your home!

If you have more questions about real estate and the Internet, contact your Realtor®. Or, you can contact Mollie at mollie@molliew.com.

4. How Much Is Your Home Really Worth?

My husband and I would like to thank you for all of your hard work in selling our Grosse Pointe Farms home, and in facilitating the purchase of our St. Clair Shores home. This is the third time we have utilized your services and have been very pleased each time. We have been impressed by your professionalism, vast knowledge of the real estate market, and your personal attention to every step of the process. We were pleased with the referrals you gave us to home inspectors and lenders. You truly are a full service Realtor®. More importantly, any prospective buyer or seller who comes in contact with you would be well served in terms of the ethics and integrity you have shown. Thank you again for a job well done.

—Peggy and Terry Valerio

When you are ready to sell your home, you and your Realtor® must determine the "asking" price for your home. This should be a combination of both the fair market value and the price that you are hoping to get for your home. Once you determine this number, you should also adjust it to make sure that you leave room to negotiate with prospective buyers. Although this sounds like we are telling you to expect to negotiate down the sales price, you should know that in some markets you may get the opportunity to negotiate up! So unlike many other purchases in this country, real estate prices should always be negotiable.

Here again is another reason to hire a Realtor®. A good, experienced Realtor® in your area will often know just by looking at your home what it can expect to fetch in the current market. Not only might they know the sale prices of similar homes that have sold in the neighborhood, but your Realtor® may know the homes' original listing prices and how much buyers in your neighborhood have been willing to negotiate.

Whether or not you decide to use a Realtor®, there are two predominant ways to determine a home's value: an appraisal and a market-value analysis. What you should expect to learn through either process is the approximate value of your home. The reality is that until your home actually sells, there is no precise way to determine exactly what your home is worth. In the business, we say that your home is worth exactly what someone pays for it. An appraiser will tell you that a home's value is equal to an amount agreed to between an able and willing buyer and an able and willing seller, when neither person is unduly influenced by outside forces.

Home Appraisal

Although an appraisal is usually done by the buyer to satisfy lending requirements, it can also be a worthwhile investment for a seller. Appraisals are commonly seen as the best way to determine your home's most precise value. In Michigan, this is called an "Opinion of Value," and can be done by a licensed broker or an appraiser. Your Realtor® can usually provide a referral to a competent one. The appraiser reviews various factors to determine the approximate sales price of your home. These factors include looking at historical records of the property and the area, looking at the property's prior sales performance, and reviewing the current condition of the property. For more detailed information on how appraisals work, contact the Appraisal Institute at 550 W. Van Buren, Suite 1000, Chicago, IL 60607, or www.appraisalinstitute.org.

There are also ways in which you as the homeowner can ensure that the appraiser looks out for your best interests. First, you should make sure that your house is in the best possible condition (see more on this in Chapter 6).

Market Value

The most common method of determining the sales price of your home is a comparative market analysis (CMA). A CMA is an estimated value of your home, based on the sales price and similar attributes of other properties in the area. CMAs may be less precise than appraisals, but they are still a reliable method for determining the asking price of your home.

It will also help if, with your Realtor®, you look at other comparable homes currently on the market in your area and compare their similarities and differences. This will help you decide the list price of your home and help you see exactly who you may be competing against for that perfect buyer.

Wynne and Doug use a program called "eNeighborhoods" which has information from the census bureau as well as recordings from the "register of deed" office. This offers the ability to go a little more in depth on property sales than what we can gather from a normal CMA.

We will generally recommend a range. You can start in the high end of that range if you are not in a hurry to sell and are more interested in maximizing your profit or net return. You would list in the low end of that range if your goal is to sell quickly.

Remember that regardless of what list price you choose, the actual sales price may be slightly higher or lower. If for some reason your house is not selling, you and your Realtor® should consider lowering the price. Beware of having your mind set on some magic number given by a CMA. Remember that these are only approximations of the real value of your home. The economy and the market can actually change in relatively short periods of time. In addition, no matter how you try to determine a price based on CMAs or appraisals, your home may have peculiarities that are just not present in any other home.

5. Selling Your Home in an Up or Down Market

Thank you for all the understanding and professionalism you displayed representing us as sellers listing our home in Algonac and representing us as buyers in the purchase of our home in Marine City. We are enjoying our new house a lot. Your professional and personal services are second to none. You will be recommended to anyone we know entering the housing market. Thanks, also, to your great assistant, Judy.

—Mark Kornago

Although the sales price may need slight modifications, regardless of the real estate market, a good Realtor® should be able to help you sell your home. This may be important to the many sellers out there who cannot wait for a market turnaround to sell. The reality is, if the house is priced fairly and your house is in a condition that appeals to the average buyer, you should be able to sell your home regardless of the market. Before we discuss price, we must mention the importance of "first strike." *You only have one chance at a "new listing."* Many agents don't understand the importance of having all your marketing tools ready at the very start. Some will put data on the MLS and days later add pictures. Not Doug. No pictures, no interest. The listing, pictures, and virtual tour must be presented to a potential buyer at the same time. Simply said, "first impresssions" are everything.

Besides the "asking" price, there are many things that can affect how quickly you sell your home, but we will start with price.

Price

For obvious reasons, the asking price will be the most important factor in determining how fast you sell your home. Despite the desire to make sure that you price your home high enough to make a profit, as well as leaving room for negotiating, you should be aware that overpricing your home is the most common and dangerous mistake that a seller can make.

A home may be overpriced for many reasons. Some sellers consider their first asking price to be a "trial balloon," where they just want to see if they can attract a better-than-normal offer. Then there are sellers who simply insist that their home is worth more than any objective market analysis indicates. For example, sellers who have been trying to sell their house themselves for months may now want to raise the price because they are paying a Realtor® for representation. That is because the sellers still want their net price, so they try to add sales commissions to the listed price. Homes like this usually stay on the market the longest and end up being sold for less than market value. One of the primary reasons so many FSBOs fail is because the seller is personally biased. It is easy to convince yourself that something you own is worth more than its real value. It's also why so many Realtors®, when selling their home, actually list with other Realtors® or at least rely on the advice of others. Objectivity is paramount.

Price and Timing Are Everything

One of our good friends, Allyson Hoffman of Northbrook, Illinois, recalls a listing that received an offer within the first few days on the market. Though it was not a full price offer, it was within a few percentage points of the asking price. The seller, despite Allyson's advice, declined the offer, believing that it was too soon to consider an offer with those particular concessions. In the end, he waited *10 months* for the next offer, resulting in *10 months* of unneeded anguish, having to keep his home in showing condition with showings occurring regularly, until ultimately, another offer was submitted that was *$40,000 less than the original offer.* It's a testimony to Allyson's professionalism that she continued to market the home all that time. Well-priced homes can, and often do, sell quickly—an infinitely more convenient situation for any seller and their family.

Remember, there are almost always a number of prospects waiting for your listing—people who have looked in your price range and neighborhood but not found the right property and want to see everything new when it comes on the market. Once those "waiters" have visited, you can typically expect showings to drop to a more regular level.

A few years ago, Ken's son and daughter-in-law asked him to help them sell their home. Since they were in another community, he referred them to a trusted Realtor® friend who knew their neighborhood well. The evening of the first day that their home was on the market, Ken got an urgent call. It seems they got 27 showings that day, and a full price offer was on the table.

"Our home was under priced," they said. "It should have been priced higher!" So, Ken carefully reviewed the information they had at hand, including the comparable sales on which the listing price was based.

"Look," he said, "you can either be greedy and risk losing a good sale, or you can simply try to understand the dynamics of a well-listed property. You are actually priced slightly higher than the comps show. And, you need to move quickly because you already have your replacement property under contract. These people were all waiting for another property in your neighborhood and in your price range. If you reject this offer, you could risk waiting weeks or months for another offer, and in the process, you could lose your new home. Or, you could take this offer, recognize that you made a healthy profit, and facilitate a smooth and easy move for you and your family." They took the offer, and in less than a month, they were ensconced in their current home. Looking back, they actually laugh at their hope to have made another few thousand dollars.

Many sellers know of a home that sold for a high price in their neighborhood, but may be unfamiliar with the particular differences between that house and their own that created a difference in value.

The bottom line is to not overprice your home. Professionals know that the longer a house is on the market, the lower the selling price is, in comparison to the asking price. In fact, after 60 days the selling price is commonly 10 percent less than the asking price, and this percentage goes up every additional month that the house is on the market. More often than not, your first offer will be your best offer. So by overpricing your home by 5 percent, you may end up losing 10 percent or more, and waiting months to sell your home.

These statistics may make you worry about whether or not you are overpricing your home. You needn't be unnecessarily concerned. If you take the time to do your homework before listing your home, you can feel confident that your home will be priced right to sell.

This leaves us with the question of how to modify the price of your home, in either an up or down market, to avoid overpricing. This is where a Realtor's® advice can be invaluable. Unlike a typical seller, who is only familiar with the markets that effect either the sale or purchase of their own homes, an experienced Realtor® will have the knowledge of many years of market changes and fluctuations. They will also have a database of sales available to expand that knowledge base. This knowledge can help turn a guessing game into an educated pricing decision.

Depending on the circumstances, you may also want to consider underpricing your home. This option can be appealing when you need to sell fast, possibly because you are moving out of the area for work, or to close on a replacement property. It is a particularly good strategy in a market where prices are falling. An underpriced property today can create an immediate reaction as opposed to becoming an overpriced property tomorrow or 30 days out when prices are lower and the home hasn't sold. In the recent past, Ken sold four properties where the buyer was the first and only party to see the property. These were cases where the buyers had difficulty finding the right property, the new listings were underpriced, and they fit the buyer's needs perfectly. Even with full-priced offers, they got bargains. Good Realtors® check for new listings every day, and when a good deal comes up, they call the buyer immediately to see the property. Underpricing can sell homes *quickly*—partly through diligent work and attention, but also as a result of a market reaction to the underpricing. This frequently results in multiple offers from competing buyers who end up paying over the asking price in order to *win* the house. Both Doug and Wynne feel that pricing a house a little lower than what a seller might expect is a good way to generate interest. Wynne was involved in a sale where an FSBO was having trouble selling a home at $99,000. They came to her and, knowing a commission was involved, wanted to re-list it at $110,000. Wynne felt it wouldn't sell at that price and kept it at the lower price. She used the MLS and her Internet savvy to market the house properly and four offers came in with a final selling price of $106,000.

It is also important to know that there are buyers in every price range in your market just waiting for the next property listing. They've already seen everything that fits their criteria without finding the "right" home. If yours is priced right and it fits the buyer's needs, you could have a quick sale. If however it is overpriced, the buyer may not see your home at all or won't make an offer, and you will lose that buyer forever.

If for some reason your house has been on the market for more than the normal amount of time in your area, action other than just lowering the price can and should be taken. If no one has even looked at your home then you can be relatively sure that price is the issue. Somehow, despite you and your Realtor's® best efforts, your home is not adequately priced for your area. It may be because of a severe "buyer's market," or it may be because many others in your area have taken less than full value for their home for one reason or another. If this is the case, making adjustments to your asking price will be necessary if you do not want to wait to sell your home.

If you have had people looking at your home, but you still have not had any reasonable offers, you should find out what specifically is discouraging buyers. There are several ways to do so. First, your Realtor® should be getting feedback from their buyers who saw your home and from other Realtors® who showed it. Not all showing Realtors® take the time to do this, but the feedback can be invaluable.

A word of caution, it is easy to get defensive when buyer feedback indicates that "the home is overpriced" or "the floor plan doesn't work." We have had sellers say, "Well, if they don't like the price, tell them to make an offer and we'll see what we can do." The fact is that most buyers, while willing to make an offer under the asking price, do not feel comfortable "lowballing" an offer. They simply feel that you are too far apart for negotiation.

A good Realtor® will seek brute honesty in feedback and will convey that to you undiluted. And while an occasional buyer may respond too personally (e.g., "what a horrid floor plan"), it's important to look at all the feedback with your Realtor® to determine your next steps.

If your home has languished on the market for several months, it may be a good time to take another look at your competition. One thing you might do is visit your competition with your Realtor®. Your Realtor® can set showings for you on properties in your price range that would be competing with your property for buyers. This could serve as a reliable reality check.

Negotiating Tools

In general terms, there are two primary approaches to negotiating a deal when price alone is the major consideration. One is to start low and know you will probably reach an agreed-on price somewhere close to the asking price. In fact, one of the jobs of your Realtor® is to try to determine your bottom line. The second approach is to make a "take it or leave it" offer. If you only want to sell at the price that you and your Realtor® have determined is fair, then this is a realistic approach to take. Then buyers will only be able to negotiate on "cosmetic" items like the closing date or what is included in the sale. Believe it or not, we had a number of deals accepted on that basis, but usually when the house was listed for slightly under the market value.

The vast majority of real estate deals, when both sides are represented, should come down to what is fair. It should end up being a win/win situation, where everyone feels satisfied with the deal. We have all dealt with buyers who "want a deal" and who are unwilling to pay fair market value for any property. They want to steal it, to stick a knife in the seller's back, and then twist it. They are only looking for someone who is vulnerable and has to sell at any price. We usually send this kind of buyer away.

Now, it is true that some deals are made this way. We have found properties that must be sold quickly to avoid bankruptcy, or that are on the verge of foreclosure. We have not hesitated to get one of our buyers into such a deal. But your Realtor® is there to protect you from buyers who take the attitude that you can only be happy if you have "screwed" the seller. This attitude is really just corruptive of the whole process of real estate sales.

So, if you haven't already, you and your Realtor® should now prepare for negotiation by formulating a game plan. You should both be clear about what is vital to the deal and what you can give up. Most bottom lines should include some unnecessary items you can give up without feeling deprived, while giving the buyers the sense they won some concessions. It is also important to understand that there are many more things to negotiate besides the price. In fact, there are occasions when price, although important in reeling a buyer in, is the *least* important negotiating objective.

For example, you may need a really quick close—you will lose a home you are trying to purchase, and you need the sale proceeds immediately. If the buyers are renters, you may not have a problem; but if they also have a house they need to sell, it may mean convincing them to own two homes for a period of time, and you may have to concede to the offering price in order to get what you need. On the other hand, you may have just put in a brand-new lighting fixture that you would love to keep, but if it means getting your asking price, it may be worth parting with. In fact, we always recommend that you remove any items that you definitely want to keep before putting your house on the market, so that you don't have to say "no" and potentially waste negotiating power on trivial items. The bottom line is that it is important to know, and to clearly communicate to your agent, those things that are important to you and those that are not.

Always try to negotiate from a position of strength. You can contribute to a stronger negotiating position by not overpricing your home. It will also help if you have taken the steps described in the next chapter to make your home as attractive as possible. And, if you are looking to buy another home, it will be to your advantage to wait until you are under contract with a buyer before you make an offer of your own.

Your Realtor® will also try to find out what might motivate the buyers. While it is not always possible to determine their motivations up front, it is usually worth trying. For example, if you find out that the buyers are moving from out of state and need extra moving time, you can give them the time they need in exchange for taking the appliances. If you are not in a hurry to move, and you can make a closing date or possession date agreeable to the buyers, don't you think they might be willing to negotiate on price?

If you find out that the buyers are being transferred and need to move quickly, are getting divorced, or are facing a termination of their rental lease, you will have accumulated information that is important to your negotiating process. Once you know as much as you can about the buyers' position, and you and your Realtor® have a clear picture of your negotiating position, you are one step closer to selling your home.

Another useful strategy in selling your home is to give the buyer a break. If negotiations are stalled, you might offer to throw in the snow blower or lawn mower, or offer to clean the carpets after you have vacated. Small gestures can be very valuable. If a buyer is on the fence, a seller who appears willing to do something extra may have the right stuff to seal a deal. And at the end of the day, that $250 used snow blower/lawn mower may have saved you an extra month's wait in selling your home. Occasionally, even offering a one-year home warranty (usually around $300–$500) can do the trick.

You may not have control over the real estate market or the sales prices in your neighborhood, but there is one area where you can personally make a huge impact. This is in the condition of your home. Making sure that your home is in the best possible condition will greatly enhance your odds of selling your home quickly and at a good price.

Ken's Homeowner Nightmare

Ken lives in ski country. Two-thirds of his properties in Summit County, Colorado are owned by nonresidents. Some of those properties are kept for the owner's occasional use, but many are rented out as investment properties. Of those, most become short-term or vacation rentals. That is, they are rented out a few nights at a time to people who are here to ski. However, many are rented long term (e.g., one-year leases) to people who either live here full-time or who come to work here a year at a time.

Being a resort community, rents (and purchase prices) are high, often beyond the means of seasonal workers. To compensate, many more people may be placed into a rental than what the property was meant for. As a result, properties are often abused, or at the very least, not very well cared for. Many renters will have pets (in addition to overstocking the property with people), even when not permitted. Carpet can be trashed, holes put in walls, cabinet doors pulled off, and so on.

Last year, Ken listed two of these properties, condominiums, in the same complex. Both being two-bedroom units, you would think that their values would be similar. After all, it was a newer complex, which appeals to many buyers. However, one owner chose to sell his property as is, while the other completely renovated his unit. Ken, of course, advised each owner of the relative values of their properties, and to a certain extent, they were priced accordingly.

The fixer-upper was priced at $260,000, while the renovated property was priced at $275,000. We felt the fixer-upper was still priced high, even though renovation costs would have been less than the difference in price between the two. And the sales proved this point.

The renovated property had an offer in the second week, and closed about a month later at only $3,000 under the asking price. The fixer-upper on the other hand, was on the market for over six months and finally sold for less than $230,000. Ken saw this property a few months later after it had been renovated by the new owners at a cost of around $10,000, and it sparkled.

That's a huge difference. It should make you think twice before you decide not to invest in making your property shine.

It is important to realize that when a potential buyer views your home, you have your one and only chance to make the right impression. You may know that the dishes are usually washed and the lawn raked, but a potential homeowner only knows what they see on that first viewing. So before you cost yourself time and money, make sure your house is "dressed and ready" for sale!

6. Dressed and Ready for Sale

> Honest, effective, reliable, and goes the extra mile. Wynne knows how to make the negotiations of the transaction come together.
>
> —Mark and Valerie Massey

Getting Ready

Buying a home can be one of the most emotional purchases a person or family makes. A buyer may see that perfect bay window with the window seat they've always dreamed of and know that your home has to be theirs. So in order to have the most successful experience in selling your home, you must appeal to the *emotions* of potential buyers.

The reality is that what your home looks like matters a lot! Deep down, most buyers want a perfect new house, regardless of what they can really afford. No matter the age of your house, your job is to make it appear as new as possible without wasting money. The point is to make your home as appealing as possible.

We always recommend to our sellers that a good place to start is with a thorough inspection. Take a pad and paper and walk from room to room, writing down what you see. Don't just focus on problem areas; look for what you should highlight. Are there wonderful French doors hidden by worn curtains? Is the fireplace blocked from view by too much old furniture? You should not only tour every room but inspect the entire property. Look at the house as if you were going to make an offer. What would you want to see? Maybe even enlist the help of an honest and impartial friend or family member to help you be more objective. If a buyer has a choice between two comparable properties that are similarly priced, they will choose the one in the best condition.

Animals Rule

Ken once had a home for sale in his market that was owned by a taxidermist. Now many people appreciate taxidermy and have no qualms about having stuffed animals on display. But there are also many people who are queasy about this. This gentleman was renowned and his home was literally filled. You could not turn a corner without having a jackal looking down on you, or a boar looking as if it was ready to attack. Ken showed this home a number of times because it was in a very nice, gated community on a fishing pond, and the home itself had a good floor plan. But every potential buyer was turned off by the animals.

Ken, along with other agents, communicated this concern to the seller via his agent (actually three agents over the course of about a year and a half), but he refused to remove the stuffed animals and heads. Perhaps he did not have a place to store them but he should have found a place, as it would have helped him sell his house immensely.

Because of the length of time it took to sell the property, while everything else in this neighborhood was being sold in days or weeks, he lost over $100,000 on the eventual sale. And this was a problem that could have been remedied easily, at little or no cost.

Dos and Don'ts

There are some very simple and inexpensive things that you can do, or that you should avoid, when you are selling your home. Remember, you have a very valuable item to sell, so—like a sophisticated salesperson—you should make sure that the product you are offering is useful and appealing. By following these 10 simple tips, you cannot only increase the sale price of your home, but hopefully ensure a quick sale.

Tip 1: Get rid of any and all clutter. Piles of books and magazines, snow globe collections and bags of recycling can be such a negative distraction that potential buyers might walk right out before passing the entry hall. The goal is to make your house spotless. The less clutter there is, the more open and spacious your home will appear, and the more likely it is that the buyer will also be able to imagine themselves and their things in your home. Too much furniture and too many knick-knacks always make a room look smaller than it is—and don't forget the garage! Remove everything off the refrigerator and reduce the personal photos around the house to *one*. Storage space is an important concern of many buyers, so the less cluttered these spaces are, the more space buyers think they are getting. Make sure there is space between each hanger in every closet to accomplish this. Don't wait until you start packing to throw out those unneeded items—now is the time to do it. Doing it now does not add work to the moving process, but simply gives you one less thing to worry about later and at the same time, adds value to the task. These things cost nothing more than time, but in the scope of a sale, they can be invaluable. There's no need to make major changes because most homeowners want to decorate themselves. You want to give buyers a spacious and clean blank canvas.

Sometimes, nothing can be more detrimental to selling a home than clutter and mess. In fact, our friend, Allyson, once listed a property that had been sitting on the market for five months for just this reason. The sellers were a young couple with two small children. As a result, the house was filled with excess furniture and toys. Allyson suggested that they rent a storage locker for the overabundant furnishings in an effort to create a greater sense of space. They listened to her and then sold the house at full price the very first day it was relisted! The most amazing part of this success story was that Allyson did *not* reduce the price upon relisting the home. The only cost on the part of the seller was their time and the minimal cost of a storage facility.

Tip 2: Avoid air fresheners. To prospective buyers, air fresheners seem like cover-ups. You are better off making sure that your home has been well aired out, particularly if you are a smoker. Try using strategic fresh flowers to add a touch of ambience as well as a fresh scent or bake fresh cookies or bread.

Tip 3: Make sure that your home is as inviting as possible. This means turning off the television and any other distracting electronic device. Instead try using soft music to set the tone. You also want inviting lighting. Make sure you have high-watt bulbs in dark rooms and soft lighting in areas where you want to detract attention.

Tip 4: Make sure that pets and children are not around when your house is being shown to prospective buyers. It is best to assume that buyers don't have pets or children and let them ask questions about how a home can accommodate their needs if necessary. The bottom line is that if a buyer is allergic to cats or dogs, your beloved pet may drive them out before giving your home a chance.

Tip 5: Avoid potentially offensive items. For example, Wynne once showed a home to a prospective buyer, Mary, a lovely lady with a quiet personality who was not just vegetarian, but vegan. She not only wouldn't eat meat, she wouldn't eat anything that came from an animal, like milk or cheese, and she would not wear leather or fur.

You can imagine her dismay when she walked into the bedroom of a nice three-bedroom, two-bathroom, split-level home, and was confronted with a picture of Ozzy Osbourne biting off a bat's head. There was no sale that day.

Since that experience, we try to preview houses first, or at least ask our homesellers to have a neutral person walk through their home to see if they have any items that might be offensive.

Tip 6: If you have furniture in less than the best condition, consider removing it (either by storing or donating it) before showing your home. Unattractive furnishings can distract potential buyers. It is usually better to have more open space than to fill it with marginal items. Also, too much furniture, or furniture that is too bulky, can make spaces seem smaller than they are.

Tip 7: If you have wood floors in good condition, be sure to show them off. Conversely, if your floors are in poor condition and you can afford it, consider having the floors refinished. If you cannot do that, you might cover any old or worn floors with clean and tidy rugs. If you have carpeting, make sure that you have it properly cleaned. In fact, stained or dirty carpet is such a huge turnoff to buyers, that depending on the condition, it may be worthwhile to replace it with inexpensive neutral carpeting. Consult with your Realtor® prior to making a decision in this area.

Tip 8: Make sure that you don't leave your car in the driveway. This is a little-known secret of the trade. When a buyer pulls in they should see the home, not your cars. Let them feel like the driveway is theirs, and maybe even visualize themselves coming home. If you can't park your car in the garage because of clutter, reread Tip 1.

Tip 9: Make sure that any important papers, prescription drugs, and valuables are put away in a safe place. The reality is that buyers are strangers that you are letting into your home. Although a Realtor® will always be there to show your home, it is best not to take chances with your private and valuable items. Besides, some buyers, such as families, go in different directions, and it is impossible for a Realtor® to monitor all individuals all the time. It is not unheard of for drug addicts to visit open houses just to steal the prescription drugs.

Having an agent present when your home is being shown adds safety and can insure that prospective buyers have all the information they need to make an offer on your home. Add your knowledgeable Realtor®, readily available to share information through good marketing, and savvy buyers will have the most likely combination of influences designed to produce the results you want.

On one occasion, while showing a home to a man and his daughter, Doug witnessed the daughter (her father was not in the room) pick up a set of what appeared to be diamond earrings from a bedroom dresser. He simply asked her if she wouldn't mind returning them. She did. And Doug never let her out of sight after that.

Tip 10: We emphasize that sellers follow what we call the *Rule of Three Cs.* Keep your home as Clean as possible, as Clutter-free as possible, and as Colorless as possible. This simple rule, when followed, will ensure that your home appeals to the greatest number of prospective buyers.

Making the Buyer Comfortable

Potential buyers may be entering their new home, and can't help but emotionally connect with the surroundings. You can take advantage of this. A fellow Realtor® and good friend, Myra Shelton, suggests making an invitation. Take a card and place it on the coffee table. Write something like, "Please sit and make yourself comfortable for a bit, as this just might be your new home. We've enjoyed living here, and I think you will too." You can also make coffee or, as mentioned earlier, bake cookies. This is not only a kind gesture, but adds pleasing, comfortable aromas.

Another useful tool is to give a list of your favorite features to your agent. This way your Realtor® can draw buyers to the best parts of your home. What made you want to buy your home is likely a selling point for prospective buyers. The more your Realtor® points out to potential buyers, the more comfortable they will feel, and the less time they will need to spend learning about the home for themselves.

One area over which you may have little control is your neighborhood. Regardless, we all know how important this factor is in buying a home. But don't fret; there are some small things you can do that can make a big difference. You can help clean up graffiti in the neighborhood; you can clean up garbage in the street; you can have the city tow away inoperative or abandoned cars. In the larger scheme, you can team up with neighbors to form a neighborhood cleanup group or a Neighborhood Watch program. Prospective buyers may be relieved to know that even though you are leaving, they are moving into a neighborhood that cares.

Most buyers are looking for a relatively modern home. As we discussed earlier, buyers want a home to appear new. Things that substantially date your house, like popcorn ceilings, metal banisters, and wood paneling, can make a sale more difficult. It may be worthwhile to look into the cost of replacing or removing these items. It may very well be a great investment.

Wynne once represented a couple, both artists, who had decorated their home with amazing artwork painted directly onto the walls throughout the house–absolutely lovely work, but definitely *not* something that would have vast market appeal. After much discussion, they finally agreed to repaint some of the most "impressive" walls white. However, they still insisted on keeping the turquoise trim surrounding the exterior of their windows. When the house didn't sell, Wynne's feedback indicated that there were still issues with the decorating and color. In response, the sellers decided to lower their price by $10,000, hoping to produce an offer. At Wynne's suggestion—"humor me," she said—they finally agreed to first repaint the turquoise trim on the outside white, a minimal expense compared to a radical price reduction. The house then sold within a week, and the sellers never had to reduce their price. They ultimately netted thousands of dollars more than they were prepared to accept.

Today's homebuyer is looking for "character." Just as popcorn ceilings are out, molding and natural woods are in. Adding molding can be a relatively inexpensive do-it-yourself project with substantial returns.

If you are going to spend money on your home, there are two places where your investment will have the greatest payback: the kitchen and the bathroom. Replacing kitchen counters and floors alone can brighten up a dated kitchen. Likewise, bathroom remodels can be moderately priced and can substantially update your home. You don't need to take any of these steps to sell your home, but be aware of what buyers will be looking for, and how you can best meet their needs. Just making your home sparkling clean can make a huge difference. Sellers must consider these factors and decide for themselves how much time and money they can invest in the final sale price of their home.

Lox and Bagels

A good friend of ours has worked with a Realtor® known in the industry as "Lox and Bagel." The nickname comes from the fact that he often "dresses" his listings for open houses, including setting the table with a lovely brunch with synthetic bagels topped with lox! Realtors® call activities such as this "staging" a home. It's often done with high-end homes, and Realtors® may even get a local furniture company to display its furniture in a new home where construction is just complete.

As silly as this sounds, this agent's houses sell, and not just because of the synthetic food. On Sunday mornings, when most of his open houses are held, he provides his guests with an idea of what it would be like to wake up to a beautiful brunch in this very home, which he hopes will soon be theirs. He even draws baths, complete with candles, champagne, and strawberries. The bottom line is that when you view his homes, you know exactly how wonderful it could be to live there. Just as in magazine or television advertising, subtleties can make a huge difference.

You may not be able to do all of the things recommended above, either for financial reasons or otherwise, but any of the steps you can take will put your home in a better selling position.

Exterior

First impressions are important, and the first thing that prospective buyers will see is the outside of your home. The exterior not only speaks for itself, but it tells potential buyers what they can expect to find inside. The reality is that if the exterior of your home is in a bad state, many buyers will just keep on driving. If you drove up to a house with peeling paint, dead plants, and falling rain gutters, you wouldn't expect the inside to be taken care of, would you? For some small things you can do to make sure that the outside of your home is as well-dressed as the inside, see our checklist at the end of the chapter.

Remember, you only get one chance to make a good first impression, and that begins with the outside of your home. So, landscaping should be groomed, walks and driveway shoveled and ice-free, toys should not adorn the lawn, and your front door should look great. Your potential buyer will have a significant amount of time to observe these things while their agent gains access to your home.

Amenities

The most common problem we see after a closing is that the seller takes an item from the property that the buyer assumed was part of the sale. This goes back to an important point that we discussed earlier; make sure that items you want to keep are removed from the house before you show it to prospective buyers. The bottom line is that there are some items that will automatically become part of the property once title is passed to the buyer, regardless of whether you assumed it was yours to keep. This is referred to as the *law of fixtures*.

The law of fixtures basically says that fixtures are part of the property and cannot be removed. Fixtures are anything that is permanently attached to the property by attachments such as bolts or screws. Some items easily fall into this definition such as counters, sinks, or flooring. But some areas are more complicated. For example, a built-in dishwasher is a fixture, because it can't just be unplugged and removed, while a refrigerator or stove is not because you can simply unplug and remove it. Similarly, window treatments are only considered fixtures if they are screwed or bolted in. So you can take curtains, but not the rod if it is bolted to the wall.

Another common area of confusion is lighting. If light fixtures are bolted to a wall or the ceiling, they are part of the sale, including expensive chandeliers and antiques. The easiest way to avoid this problem is by removing these items (and replacing them with inexpensive fixtures) before showing your home. This is much more serious than removing items that a buyer may dislike, because if you show them, they become part of the transaction. Unlike nonfixtures (refrigerators, washers, and dryers), a buyer does not even have to request these items in the contract.

If your home has a dated stove or refrigerator and you plan to buy new ones for your next home, it may be worthwhile to buy them before you show your home. This runs slightly counter to the rule that you shouldn't show items that you intend to keep, but here there is a good reason. Think of your kitchen as a showroom. Unlike lighting fixtures, buyers generally know that these appliances are not necessarily included in the sale. Nice appliances can show prospective buyers how contemporary and updated your kitchen can look. Dated appliances really make a kitchen look old. Even if your buyers insist on keeping the appliances, if you make sure that you are compensated, it may still ensure a quicker sale at a better overall price.

Real Problems

There may be some real problems with your house that need to be repaired before you sell it. Except in a tight market, major "as-is" fixer-uppers are hard to sell. In fact you should never spend money on cosmetic repairs unless you know that your home is structurally sound. If there are genuine problems with your home, you should either spend the money to address them, or understand that you will have to sell it as a fixer-upper for a reduced price.

Leaks Don't Lie

Ken's Story

Some years ago, before I was a Realtor®, I was a private investigator. I received a call from an attorney who represented the Gordons, a couple who had recently bought a great old home in a higher-end Denver subdivision. This was always a popular "moving up" area of Denver and is known for a certain degree of wealth and status, though the residences there are not ostentatious.

It seems the Gordons, during the moving-in process, filled the garage with dozens of boxes that contained an old and rare book collection they had been adding to for years. The first weekend after they had moved in, before they finished unpacking, there was a rainstorm. Colorado is known for its summer "gully washers," rainstorms that may last for only half an hour or so but dump tremendous amounts of rain and literally "wash out" the gullies, curbs, and drainage systems. This was a true gully washer.

The Gordons never anticipated what would happen during that storm. It rained inside the garage, destroying a significant amount of their rare book collection along with lots of other household items. The Gordons were away at the time, so the situation progressed unimpeded. They were devastated when they returned home.

Of course, they had a professional home inspection when they were under contract to purchase the home, and the inspector did not indicate the presence of any roof leaks. They contacted their agent, who had recommended the inspector, and asked for assistance. She contacted the sellers' agent, who professed no knowledge, then purportedly contacted the seller, who also claimed innocence. The Gordons, in their extreme frustration, hired an attorney, who contacted me to conduct a thorough investigation.

The resulting lawsuit named several people: the sellers, the sellers' agent, the home inspector, the buyers' agent, and the two brokers. The following sections reveal why each person was culpable.

The Sellers

My investigation revealed that the sellers had experienced roof leaks as a matter of course for several years. It was a Spanish-style tile roof and very expensive to repair or replace. I had located the roofing company that had performed repairs to the roof through the years. I obtained a statement from the owner of the company that, two years prior to the sale, he had told the sellers that he refused to do any more repairs to the roof because the patchwork was not working. The roof needed to be replaced. That disclosure to the sellers was also in writing from the roofing company. The sellers' Property Disclosure, given to the buyers during the contract period, indicated that the roof was sound and had no leaks.

The Sellers' Agent

The sellers' agent was well known. She'd been in business for many years and had a reputation for specializing in high-end listings in this neighborhood. She was known for staging her homes so that they would sell quicker. That is, she would instruct her sellers to paint and do other cosmetic work to make the house look its best, and she would even lend expensive furniture when it would help make the home look luxurious. When I met with her and her broker, she denied any knowledge of roof leaks or other problems pertaining to the house. I was able to determine, however, that she had instructed the sellers to paint parts of the interior of the home. I later learned from other sources that she had specifically noted water stains on living room walls, dining room walls, and other walls, and ordered them all to be painted so the water stains would not be noticed by visiting prospective buyers.

The Home Inspector

Before meeting with the original home inspector, I hired another, and we went through the home in some detail. Among other things, we noted that in the attic, the sellers had placed sheets of plastic, each of which showed dried watermarks. It was clear that the sheets of plastic were meant to capture water leaking from the roof. When I interviewed the home inspector, he admitted that he had never gone into the attic (even to inspect the insulation). He also admitted he had no money and no insurance and didn't even own a home. He said, "So sue me. I'll just go out of business." In fact, he was not bonded or insured and didn't even have any formal training.

The Buyers' Agent

Of all the parties, this woman was the most innocent. She truly felt she had done her job and was straightforward in her interview with me. She was also fairly new in the business, with little more than a year of experience at the time she worked with the Gordons. However, she had made a serious mistake. She had recommended a home inspector without having checked out his credentials or reputation. The simple action of checking with her broker or other agents in her office to make sure her buyers had a truly professional inspector could have prevented this entire incident despite the efforts on the parts of the sellers and their agent to hide the evidence.

The Brokers

Regardless of the direct liability and culpability of the agents involved, they work for, and are under the supervision of their brokers. In both cases, the brokers either failed to train their agents properly or failed to supervise their actions effectively. Hence, they were named in the lawsuit as well. In fact, this is another good reason to work with a Realtor®. They must, under Colorado law, be covered by errors and omissions insurance, and many brokers have umbrella coverage as well.

The Result

The Gordons won their lawsuit. However, it took more than a year, and in the meantime, they had to finance a complete roof replacement on their own. It was difficult to accurately ascertain the value of the rare books they lost, so the amount they collected for lost goods was far less than what they felt they should have gotten. Of course, they received no compensation for the psychological pain and suffering they endured, nor for the time lost from work pursuing the lawsuit. So, in spite of the fact that some justice was eventually served, no one came out a true winner, and the entire mess could have been avoided with good representation and a little dose of honesty.

If you suspect that your home has serious issues such as structural damage, termites, mold, sink-holes, lead paint, radon, flood damage or a wet basement, you should start with your own home inspection. A visual inspection will help you pinpoint potentially serious issues so that you can have them assessed by a specialist.

You should also be aware that once you know about defects, you are legally obligated to disclose them to potential buyers. You and your agent must disclose any *known* material defects in your property. Of course, if you are selling your house "as is" the buyer must accept any conditions as part of the sale, they still must be fully disclosed.

Doug's Story

A few years ago, one of Doug's clients, Tim, listed a rather old Queen Anne–style home that had been in his family for generations. He had recently inherited the home and wasn't particularly interested in fixing it up or living in it, so he decided to put it on the market. He informed his original Realtor®, whom we'll call Joe, that he didn't know much about the condition of the house, but that he did remember that the bathroom on the second floor had flooded a few years before, leaking through the ceiling, and eventually damaging two of the downstairs bedrooms. Because the carpet had been replaced and the walls repainted, there was no visible sign of the incident.

Joe advised Tim not to say anything to avoid scaring away potential buyers. Taking Joe's advice, he accepted a full-price offer and never made any mention of the water damage.

During the inspection, the water damage was discovered and the buyers not only backed out, but they threatened both Tim and Joe with lawsuits for failing to disclose known damage to the property.

As it turned out, Tim came to Doug's office. He not only helped Tim with the mess that Joe had created, but he put his family home back on the market with full disclosure of the water damage, and listed it for only $10,000 less than the original asking price. Although it took a few months to sell, Doug finally sold the home to a handyman and his wife because they knew that they could make the necessary repairs for under $3,000 and were happy to have saved some money! There is always a buyer for every home; the important thing is finding the *right* buyer.

Insurance

As long as you plan to sell your home, you need to make sure the home is insurable.

Recently, a Realtor® friend reported receiving a termination notice from her insurance company. She had been insured with the same company for more than 25 years and had never filed a claim. However, the insurance company just found out that she lived more than ten miles from a fire station.

Another Realtor® friend received a notice from one of his sellers who had recently listed a home for sale. The notice included a copy of a letter received from his insurance company. His insurance was being canceled because his home was on the market for sale; the insurance company stated that having one's home for sale presented greater risk due to the fact that strangers would be going through it.

It should be noted that the National Association of REALTORS® (NAR) and its state associations are fighting for legislation that would prevent such arbitrary rules by insurance companies.

Any property you purchase that requires financing will also require hazard insurance, otherwise known as homeowner's insurance. Your lender will not provide financing without it. If you are purchasing a condominium, townhouse, or other property that is considered a *common interest community,* this section may not apply. If the property has a homeowners' association that provides insurance on all the units, you will not have to purchase your own. But you should purchase insurance for your possessions, sometimes known as a "condo policy."

Insurance covers you for a number of things, the most disastrous of which is the total loss of your home by fire or other calamity. Homeowner's insurance also provides you with liability coverage in the event that someone is injured on your property, and it covers you in the event of loss from theft or other smaller mishaps. Interestingly, however, some of the things that most dramatically affect homeowners are being decreased or eliminated from insurance coverage, such as coverage for mold and water leaks. As of this writing, we face a national insurance crisis.

The recurring theme of alarm in national, state, and local meetings of Realtors® centers on the growing insurance crisis. More and more people are discovering that hazard insurance is hard to find or nonexistent. There are three primary reasons that insurance companies are refusing to underwrite insurance on new purchases:

1. The seller has either filed a claim, or simply called about a problem, and the insurance company no longer wishes to insure or reinsure the home. The current seller's insurance could refuse to renew or the refusal could come from a different company that has been contacted by the seller or buyer. The property may have had water problems, whether from leaky roofs, broken pipes, or runoff, and the insurance company feels it may happen again or the property may have mold. The interesting thing is that the homeowner may not have even filed a claim. They may simply have called to see if a situation were covered and if they should file a claim. But overall, companies feel that properties that have experienced past claims are more likely to experience future claims. The property now becomes, for all practical purposes, uninsurable.

2. The buyer may have had claims on a prior residence that makes the buyer, in the eyes of insurance underwriters, uninsurable. It could be because of similar problems noted above. It could be because a company had to pay a claim because the buyer's previous home was poorly maintained. Overall, companies state that buyers who have filed past claims are more likely to file future claims. Whatever the reason, the buyer becomes uninsurable.

3. The buyer may have low credit scores. What do low credit scores have to do with homeowner's insurance? Insurance companies have started to underwrite based on their assessment of a buyer's ability to properly maintain their home. In their estimation, people with low credit scores usually are

unable to afford routine maintenance, leading the home to fall into disrepair and hence leading to claims-related damage.

Insurance companies claim a number of reasons for the current crisis. They point to the $40+ billion in losses resulting from the terrorist attacks of September 11, 2001, and to major losses from natural disasters, such as hurricane Katrina. They point to the surge of mold-related claims and call attention to aggressive low pricing in the past that resulted in major losses. What they do not point to, but studies have shown may be the actual reason for their loss of profits, are the losses they have suffered on their stock market investments.

The warning is clear: you can no longer take property insurance for granted. As of right now, the past traditional concept of automatic insurance is outdated! You must apply for and obtain homeowner's insurance at the earliest possible date in a transaction. Then, if denied by one company, there is at least time to shop for other coverage. You might also seek out an insurance broker who works with multiple lines. A broker would have a better idea of where to place an application based on either credit scores or claims history.

What Is a C.L.U.E. Report?

A claims history report on a seller's residence (called C.L.U.E. for Comprehensive Loss Underwriting Exchange) can be obtained from ChoicePoint, an online identification and credential verification service. Through their ChoiceTrust program, they manage and maintain information about claims filed on properties in the United States (www.choicetrust.com). The report will show all claims filed in the past five years, including the nature and amount of each settlement. Examples could range from water or fire damage to dog bites. About 90 percent of all insurers nationally participate in C.L.U.E.

and a good insurance broker will most likely know those that don't.

C.L.U.E. reports are available on properties, not individuals, so when a buyer makes an offer on a property, they will have a clause requiring you to obtain a C.L.U.E. report. It will cost you approximately $20, and you can pay and download the report online or request it by mail. If you find your home is uninsurable, it's much better to know in advance so you have time to check insurability with other companies. Mortgage lenders require insurance, so if you are stuck with a property that is uninsurable, you will most likely have to attract a cash buyer to purchase the home.

Insist as a counter to any offer, that the buyer immediately contact a lender and have them check the buyer's insurance scores to make sure they are not at risk of being unable to obtain insurance (see #3 above). And once an offer becomes a contract, make sure the buyer applies for and obtains insurance immediately. If they have been denied coverage and received a letter from an insurance company, they can obtain a free copy of their insurance scores for review from ChoicePoint.

The point to emphasize is that you should obtain a C.L.U.E. report immediately upon listing your property for sale. Then, you will either have time to address any problems that come up, or relax with the knowledge that there will be no concerns that could prevent a sale.

This issue of insurance has become so important that the National Association of REALTORS® has appointed an insurance task force to address the growing problem. The task force has already put forth recommendations for state associations to begin working on legislation, to educate their members, and to discover other ways of handling the problem.

Resort Homes

Sorry, but Ken cannot leave this section without a brief discussion of resort homes and the special needs facing sellers of these properties. Many properties in resort markets are owned by nonresidents; therefore, it becomes absolutely crucial that you have representation. A good Realtor® can advise you of the condition of a property (which you may not have actually seen for some time); help coordinate professional services for repairs and renovations; arrange professionals to help with such problems as inaccurate surveys and incursions by neighboring properties onto yours or of your property onto another; and a myriad of other services not normally performed by Realtors® in most metropolitan areas.

In addition, the national economy may not have the same affect in resort areas as it does in metropolitan areas. Good professional advice is important to understanding your options.

Checklist for Home Preparation

Begin With the Exterior

1. Keep the lawn mowed. A well-manicured lawn, neatly trimmed shrubs, and cleanly swept sidewalks create a good first impression.

2. Be sure to fertilize your grass to make it look lush and green.

3. Trim or cut back overgrown shrubs.

4. Paint the house if necessary. (If you do decide to paint your house, drive through new neighborhoods and choose a contemporary,

neutral color. Don't paint your house the same old color it was in 1970.)

5. Clean stains and oil from sidewalks and driveways. A badly stained driveway suggests that the house may not have been well maintained.

6. Replace cracked or broken windows and torn screens.

7. Hose down the entrance of your house to get rid of annoying cobwebs and dead bugs.

8. Make sure the entry light and doorbell are in good working order.

9. Inspect the roof and gutters. Make repairs and paint as necessary.

10. Repaint the front door. A new coat of paint suggests a well-cared for home.

11. Put a fresh coat of paint on your mailbox.

12. Be sure driveways and sidewalks are free of ice and snow in the winter.

13. Place a pot of fresh flowers by the front door or along the walk.

Now Let's Look at the Interior

1. Begin with a full housecleaning from top to bottom. Clean out closets and throw away unused items. Make sure that clothes are hung neatly and shoes are tidily arranged. Eliminating clutter makes your home look more spacious.

2. Make sure the walls are clean and free of smudges and fingerprints. Give them a fresh coat of paint if washing doesn't do the trick.
3. Arrange furniture to make your rooms appear more spacious. Get rid of badly worn furniture or place it in storage.
4. Wash the windows, inside and out!
5. Wash the curtains.
6. Clean the carpets and wax the floors.
7. Repair any sticking doors.
8. Fix leaky faucets and clean the water stains from the sinks, toilets, and shower doors.
9. Replace burned-out lightbulbs and make sure that all light fixtures are in good working order.
10. The kitchen is the most important room in your house. Make it bright and inviting. Wash the walls and cabinets or give them a new coat of paint if necessary. Clean the vent hood. If the floor is badly worn, consider replacing it.
11. Make the bathrooms sparkle! Repair old caulk in showers and tubs. Place fresh towels in the bathrooms.
12. Clean the bedrooms and replace faded curtains and bedspreads.
13. Clean the basement and the garage. Get rid of items you no longer use or put them in storage. Make sure there is plenty of light in the basement.

14. If the basement is dark and gloomy, consider giving the walls and floor a coat of white paint.
15. Make sure your house smells fresh and clean. Nothing is a bigger turn off to a buyer than a smelly dog bed or dirty litter box.
16. If there is a wood-burning fireplace, have the chimney cleaned. This is not only a safety measure—soot has an odor!

7. Screening Prospective Buyers

A career move brought me to Michigan and once I learned I would be relocating, I began the real estate website cruise. I came across Doug and Kathie's and was immediately impressed. I emailed them my needs and an immediate response by Doug led to his devoting an entire weekend to me and my search. His knowledge, professionalism, candor, and responsiveness resulted in my finding a beautiful home. Finding a home for me is not where Doug and Kathie stopped. They have assisted me in countless home-related needs. They truly define *added value* in real estate today.

—Sharon Gjertsen

Motivation

The motivation for selling your home will be a substantial factor in determining the kind of buyers you are looking for. For example, if you need to sell your home because you have been offered a job in a new state, you may be willing to look for a broader range of buyers than if you are merely selling in order to buy a bigger home. Likewise, a buyer looking for an investment property may want different things than one who is looking for a home for their family. Knowing both your motivation and the motivation of your prospective buyers can help the negotiating process. There are many types of buyers, with many different financial backgrounds, and sometimes a buyer with a

3 percent down payment or less can be just as good as an all-cash buyer.

Conventional Financing

When selling your home, you will likely be familiar with some of the basics of financing based upon your own experiences as a buyer. However, there are some important aspects of financing that you should know to ensure that your perfect buyer can actually afford your home. How the buyer intends to pay for your home, and whether or not they are qualified for financing, is really the most important aspect of the entire sales transaction. We all know that without the money, there is no sale.

There are three primary sources for financing the purchase of a home: banks and credit unions, mortgage bankers, and mortgage brokers. Most people are aware that banks and credit unions loan money for home purchases, including the former Savings and Loan Associations. Savings and Loans, banks, and credit unions lend money directly to the buyer from their own pool of funds, usually based on customer deposits. The individuals who work for the bank are usually called "loan officers." Loan officers are often paid commission in addition to their salary, which provides their incentive to get loan applications.

Mortgage bankers are also direct lenders and use their own funds, or those of wealthy investors, but they usually do not keep the loan. They will often sell the loan after the sale of a property to a government-sanctioned major home lender like Freddie Mac or Fannie Mae. You might not even know if your loan is sold off, as mortgage bankers often continue to service a loan by mailing statements and collecting payments.

Mortgage brokers do the loan shopping for the buyer, searching for the lender with the program or interest rate that fits their client's situation. They take the application and can apply to dozens of lenders like banks and mortgage bankers, and act as intermediaries between borrowers and lenders. They can't control interest rates or terms and are usually paid by both the buyer and the lender through closing fees or points. The points paid to buy the loan are often the same as going directly through the lender. One point equals one percent of the loan amount. Regardless of whether a buyer uses a broker or a banker, the key is making sure that your buyer is financially qualified to purchase your home.

Prequalification and Preapproval

The terms *prequalification* and *preapproval* are often used by buyers and their agents, and it can be important that you know the difference between them. A prequalification letter says the buyer earns enough money to buy a home in a certain price range, and this letter usually means that the lender has checked the buyer's credit. It may or may not mean that the buyer's income or available funds have been verified. It would be important to insist on receiving a prequalification letter from the buyer's lender that includes such verification. What a prequalification letter does not include is actual loan approval.

If a buyer has a preapproval letter, the lender has checked the buyer's credit, and has verified information on their income, debts, and available funds. It also means that the buyer's loan package has been submitted for loan underwriting. That means that the ultimate investor has reviewed the file and approved the loan *subject to certain conditions*. These conditions would usually include such things as a receipt of a contract to purchase a home within the approved purchase amount and a satisfactory appraisal of the home. There may also be a time limit on the approval. It could also include such things as receipt of a current bank statement or payroll stub. Most homes go under contract with a prequalification letter or a requirement to produce it within a certain number of days. However, a preapproval letter simply demonstrates that the buyer is better prepared and is able to offer conditional proof that they can purchase your home.

When you enter into a contract with a buyer there will likely be a deadline by which they must have full loan approval. If they do not obtain full loan approval by the contract deadline, the buyer may terminate the contract. If the buyer does not terminate the contract, they will be obligated to purchase the home or lose their earnest money deposit. This ensures that your interests are protected.

Prequalification Letter

The following is the prequalification clause that we usually insist on including in offers to purchase received on behalf of our sellers:

Buyer shall provide Seller, within ____ calendar days from acceptance of this contract, with a prequalification letter from the lender or its representative showing that: (i) Buyer has made full and complete written loan application; (ii) Lender has reviewed Buyer's credit, application, and financial information, and, subject to verification and customary underwriting requirements, Buyer has adequate down payment, closing costs, and residual funds to consummate this purchase, and is qualified for the new loan specified in Section 4b of this contract. If Buyer fails to provide Seller with this prequalification letter, Seller may terminate this contract by giving written notice to Buyer within ten business days of the deadline set forth in this section.

Creative Financing

Buyers that have trouble getting financing through the normal programs may need to get creative. Some ideas our borrowers like are the NIV loan or no-doc loan. With enough money down, usually 20 percent but sometimes only 10 percent, buyers can get one of these loans. NIV stands for "no income verification." It is a loan where the lender feels there is a large enough down payment, and hence they would feel relatively secure if you were to default, that they don't concern themselves with verifying the income stated on the loan application. The lender may simply verify that the buyer is employed and that they actually have the resources necessary to cover the down payment and closing costs. A no-doc loan is a loan where the lender does not require documentation of either income or assets (assets in this case being the money to cover down payment and closing costs). Both of these loans will have a somewhat higher interest rate. But when buyers can't secure normal financing, these are still good loans to go after.

Many Realtors® have also identified certain people who have money to invest, and who would like to earn somewhat more than the prevailing 30-year treasury rate. For 1 percent or 2 percent above the current 30-year rate, they are often willing to finance a smaller mortgage themselves. Sometimes such loans have balloon payments, meaning that after a period of smaller payments (perhaps five years), the entire amount becomes due. For people who have had credit problems but can demonstrate they are making efforts to clean up their credit, a loan such as this will often get them to the point where they can get conventional refinancing long before a balloon payment becomes due. When a buyer has very little cash to put down, a private lender may take other collateral instead, such as cars or business equipment.

There are many types of creative financing. All of them carry more risk to the buyer than normal conventional financing, and most will cost more in terms of interest rates. But there is really no risk to you as long as the buyer has been preapproved. When you are looking for the right buyer, knowing that they have secured financing, even if it is through unconventional means, will ensure that your sale will be successful. Sometimes it's the only way to make a deal work, and, if so, you shouldn't be afraid to sell to someone who is using creative financing. Just make sure you ask a lot of questions and have your Realtor® at your side.

8. Closing the Deal

Communication was the key to closing the sale in less than 90 days. Wynne, thank you so much.

—Lynn and Agnes Klettner

Once a potential buyer has decided that they are interested in purchasing your home, their agent will prepare the actual offer, called an *offer to purchase real estate*. The contract will then be submitted to you through your agent to be evaluated. The potential buyer will present you with a deposit, also called *earnest money,* to signify that they are serious about buying the home, intend to perform as promised under the offer, and will come to closing with the balance of the money needed to close the purchase. Some Realtors® place a great deal of importance on the amount of earnest money presented with the offer and feel the more earnest money presented, the better the buyer is.

As the seller, you have the final determination whether or not to accept an offer. In the best of worlds, you will find a buyer that has enough money, is highly qualified, and even submits more earnest money to show that they are very interested in your home. But in reality, there are often good buyers who may be first-time homebuyers, who are getting a low–down payment or nothing-down loan, or are borrowing the earnest money to submit with the offer. We have submitted offers for first-time homebuyers with a promissory note as the earnest money. This is when the buyer promises to bring the money to closing, usually out of loan proceeds. We have also submitted offers with minimal earnest money; usually 1 percent of the purchase price is about the least acceptable deposit. It is then incumbent on your Realtor®

to determine whether minimal earnest money represents a deterrent to the buyer's ability to purchase your home.

The buyer's agent may want to include one or more "extra" clauses in the contract to cover special requests. For example, they may want to have the carpet professionally steam cleaned prior to closing, and a paragraph in the contract could ask for that. If the buyer is purchasing land on which to build a home, they would probably want to know if a survey, soil tests, or other information is available. Again, a clause would be inserted to cover that need. There are so many clauses, and so many special requests by buyers, that to cover them all would be impossible.

Once the offer is submitted to you, there are three possible responses: (1) you can accept the offer as submitted and sign it, putting you both under contract; (2) you can counter the offer, changing the price or other terms in the contract; or (3) you can outright reject the offer.

Once you have accepted the offer without question, do not try to second guess the process. It is not the time to worry if you accepted too little or gave up too much. If you've done your homework, and you got what you wanted in the deal, be happy. The buyer probably has an agent smart enough to advise them that the offer meets your needs and that it was not worthwhile trying to squeeze more out of it.

It is absolutely ridiculous, however, to refuse to respond to a legitimate offer. Hopefully, your Realtor® will not let you ignore a good offer. Recently, one of our sellers had a property on the market at $179,000 and an offer came in at $163,000. Our seller reacted to the offer as though it was insulting and said she would not even respond. This was from a woman who regularly made very low offers on properties when she was the buyer. We told her that ignoring the offer was not an option; she hired us to sell her property and part of our responsibility is to communicate with every potential buyer until they either buy the property or go away. She said, "Fine, then tell them I'm holding out for full price." We did. Within an hour, the same buyer submitted a new offer at $176,000, and the seller accepted. There are, however, agents who forget their objectivity, become emotionally involved, and take offers personally. When reviewing a buyer's low offer, we've had listing agents tell us, with all the resentment they can muster, "This is an insult. My seller won't even respond to this." The agent should realize that they are not the seller, *you* are. If there is a viable buyer who wants the property and is capable of buying it, they will run the risk of losing a sale for you.

Finally, although most rejected first offers elicit a counterproposal from the buyer, you should beware. Often the first offer is the best offer. The negotiating process continues until you and the buyers have come to an agreement on the price, terms, inclusions, and exclusions which work for both of you, or both parties decide they've gone as far as they are willing, and will go no further. If the agents and their clients have done their work responsibly, it should be a deal that makes everyone satisfied, even happy. It will be a win/win deal for everyone.

Once you and the buyer have agreed on terms and signed, it becomes a contract between the two of you. A contract is simply an agreement between two or more people (called *parties*) to do certain things, and in exchange, some form of compensation is paid. In this case, when you and the buyer do what you have agreed to do in the contract, the house will be transferred to the buyer, and you will get the money.

Some of Your Responsibilities Are to:

- provide the buyer with a property disclosure, which is your best representation of the condition of the property and all the fixtures that will be sold to the buyer;

- provide a lead-based paint disclosure (for properties constructed prior to 1978);
- provide a square-footage disclosure (which is your best representation as to the size of the home), along with your source for that information;
- let the buyer know if there are any material defects with the property (required by most state laws);
- provide the buyer with a title commitment or an abstract of title;
- provide the buyer with declarations and bylaws, covenants and restrictions, homeowners' association financial documents, or any other documents that pertain to any homeowners' association or neighborhood that might have some say as to what you can and cannot do with your home;
- let the buyer and certain other people have access to the home for purposes of conducting a home inspection, an appraisal, taking measurements, and so forth;
- answer the buyer's legitimate questions about the house; and
- show up at the appointed time to sign the documents to transfer title of the property to the buyer. (In resorts, this is often done by overnight delivery of documents.)

Some of the Buyer's Responsibilities Are to:

- apply for a mortgage loan (if needed) and provide all the information required by the lender to process that loan;

- get the money necessary to close the purchase—down payment and closing costs;
- provide, and usually pay for, an appraisal to determine the current market value of the property (this is separate from the appraisal that you may have paid for yourself, earlier in the process, to determine the best selling price for your home);
- conduct an inspection of the property, usually with the help of a professional home inspector;
- review the title and other documents provided by you and your Realtor® and determine if they are acceptable; and
- show up at the appointed time to take title to the property and pay you the money for your home—the closing.

Contingencies

Nearly every contract has contingencies that give one party or the other the right to cancel the contract if certain things about the property are not satisfactory to that party or certain obligations of the other party are not met. For example, the loan contingency clause requires the buyer to apply for a mortgage by a certain date and to get loan approval by another specific date. If the buyer's lender anticipates problems getting loan approval, it will be up to the buyer to cancel the contract by the loan approval deadline. In that event, the property will go back on the market. The buyer has the right to review the title and association documents, and if the buyer finds those documents unacceptable, they can cancel the contract and buy another property. Let's look at some of the major contingencies included in nearly every home purchase contract.

The buyer normally has the right to conduct an inspection of your home to determine its condition and everything included in the sale. This contingency gives the buyer the right to ask you to remedy things that may reduce the value of the home, and to terminate the contract if you can't reach an agreement on payment for potential repairs.

Other contingencies can also be built into an offer, the inclusion of which will depend on a variety of circumstances. For example, perhaps the buyer must sell their current home before they will have the money to purchase your home. In this case, they will want a contingency stating that if they cannot sell their existing home, they can terminate your contract. If you are willing to accept such a contingency, you should use it as a bargaining tool—maybe in exchange for taking the home as is—and you should impose a definite time limit. You can also give the buyers a seventy-two hour right of refusal to buy the house without contingencies and then put the house back on the market to see if there are any better buyers out there.

If there are special problems with the property, the buyer may want to engage your efforts to have those problems removed, and they will make their offer contingent on the successful resolution of those problems. For instance, if a neighbor has an outbuilding or driveway that encroaches on your property, they may ask you to take the necessary steps to eliminate the encroachment. Because you may already have an established relationship with your neighbors, it might be easy for you to accomplish, making the buyer happy at a very small cost. Often, conditions like this may not be discussed until the buyer has received and reviewed the title documents. While title documents address these issues in general, the buyer may want to amend the contract to specifically address those things they want resolved as a condition of going forward.

Inspection

If you are selling a condominium in a newer development, the buyer may feel comfortable conducting the home inspection themselves. Some of our buyers have plugged a hair dryer into all the electrical outlets to make sure they were working; ran the dishwasher; turned on all the burners on the stove; tried the oven; ran water in all sinks, baths, and toilets to make sure there were no leaks; and checked for other details that could be inspected by observation. Particularly in older properties, many use professional home inspectors, and they have a right to do so on any property. The buyer and their Realtor® will review the condominium documents to determine the responsibilities of the homeowners' association. For example, if heat is included in the dues, the association is generally responsible for maintaining heating systems. It is also generally responsible for outside maintenance, including painting, roof replacement, maintenance of common facilities such as a pool or clubhouse, and so on. But if the heating system is separate for each condominium, and the individual homeowners are responsible, then the buyer may also inspect the heating system. In that case, the buyer might need a professional.

A good home inspector has been trained in all the systems and details that make up a house. A good home inspection will take from a couple of hours to a full day, depending on the size and complexity of your house. Make sure the buyers know important positive facts, such as the roof being replaced last year rather than an inspector guessing that it is five or six years old. Inspectors are not perfect, and the reality is that their inspections are mostly based on visual perceptions.

At the completion of the inspection, the inspector may take the buyer through the home to emphasize what might need attention. Those are things the buyer may want to discuss with you and your Realtor®. The buyer may ask you to remedy some or all of those items. Hopefully, the buyer's agent will inform them not to "sweat the small stuff." For example, if all the buyer finds in the home inspection is a bathtub or two that need caulking, furnace filters that need changing, an outside door that needs a new weather seal, or some other minor details, the buyer should agree to do the repairs themselves once they move in. However, occasionally the inspector will discover a condition that requires a specialist. For example, they may find a cracked foundation wall that could be due to something more than normal settling. In that case, they might recommend the buyer have a structural engineer inspect the foundation. Other serious issues, from the chimney to the furnace, may require different specialists.

It would be appropriate for the buyer to request that you correct any major problems. If the heat exchanger on the furnace has a leak, it must be replaced, which can be costly. If any appliances do not work, the buyer may ask that they be repaired or replaced. If the roof is in such disrepair or so old that replacement is imminent, the buyer may ask you to have it replaced prior to completing the sale. Keep in mind, however, that regardless of their Realtor's® advice, many buyers will want everything fixed, even minor items.

When the buyer makes these requests, you can respond in a variety of ways. You can agree to have the problems remedied prior to closing, if you think that the cost to you is reasonable in relation to the sales price. You can refuse on the grounds that the price the buyer negotiated on the house does not leave you enough money to make the corrections. Or you may offer to settle with the buyer somewhere in between. If you do not have the cash to fix the furnace, for example, but recognize that it needs repair, you can offer to compensate the buyer at closing, and let the buyer have it repaired after the home is theirs. As long as you and the buyer can resolve the inspection items to your mutual satisfaction, and you put the agreement in writing, you can proceed to closing. If you cannot resolve the issues, and the inspection is a contingency in the contract, the buyer can cancel the contract and move on. And even if the buyer asks for minor items to be addressed, you should seriously consider whether you are willing to lose the contract rather than address the items. Sometimes, half a day with a handyman can make everyone happy.

On the other hand, we've had more than one seller for whom we negotiated one or more backup offers, sometimes for more than the original contract. Consequently, the seller was able to refuse all inspection requests, knowing he had other buyers waiting in line.

You should also make sure that you are *not* there when the inspector goes through. One seller lost $1,700 because the inspector put his head under the sink for thirty seconds too long and the seller blurted out, "Oh, I was going to fix that anyway." But it turned out to be more of a problem than the seller had anticipated. Had the seller not said anything it might have been overlooked, or the buyer might not have asked for the repair. Honesty is a good thing, but don't compromise when you don't have to.

Title Documents and Easements

The contract will describe certain documents that you are obligated to provide to the buyer, either in the form of a title commitment or an abstract of title. Whichever form it takes, it is a legal picture of the title to the property. It shows who owns the property (hopefully, you), the existing mortgage company, and the initial amount of your loan. Also, it shows other things about the property that need to be cleared up prior to closing or that might impede the buyer's ability to purchase the home.

The buyer and their agent will review these documents to ensure there are no title problems that would prevent the buyer from getting clear title to the property. For example, if there are liens or obligations against the property, which total more than the purchase price, the buyer would have a right to inquire how those debts are going to be paid. Typically, buyers do not want to take title of a property that has obligations against it which cannot be cleared by the title company at closing. It might be that some of the obligations shown in the title documents have actually been paid, but the payments have not been recorded with the county clerk. A simple recording of the documents would clear those debts.

Some problems disclosed in a title search may be very simple to remedy. For example, if the title is shown to be held in the names of both a husband and wife as joint tenants, but one has died, a simple recording of the death certificate will remove that person from the title, enabling the surviving spouse to transfer title to the buyer.

There are also things on virtually every set of title documents that will remain with the property even after sale. Utility companies that have power, sewer, water, and cable lines running to the property will generally have a continuing easement to go onto the land for purposes of repair, replacement,or installation of utilities. This is limited to the areas designated on the *plat,* the surveyor's exact drawing of the homesite.

An easement is not an actual title to or ownership of property. It is simply a recorded agreement giving access to another person or entity for limited purposes. Local governments might have easements for a variety of reasons, such as access to power poles. Some states may require homeowners in certain communities to set aside extra land to dump snow off the roadway, or in beach communities to allow for public access to the waterfront. An easement may give a neighbor the right to cross your property to get to their own, or to share a driveway if they are otherwise unable to get reasonable access to their home. Or, the buyer may have an easement across a neighbor's land. Easements are very common and should not deter a buyer from purchasing your home. If they have an experienced Realtor®, they should already be informed of this fact.

Neighborhood and Condo Associations

Until the 1960s, neighborhoods were established and communities grew without a lot of community planning. In older cities, you will often find that types of homes in one neighborhood are very different from one another. You may find a ranch house next to a modern house, or a shack next to a mansion. In the mountains you often see an A-frame next to a large traditional-style house. Commercial, residential, and industrial components can be randomly interspersed. Over time, governing authorities (town councils and county governments) often developed rules and regulations that gave them the authority to approve what was (and is) built, to ensure that some consistency exists in each neighborhood development and to designate how homes, stores, and industrial development are separated.

Restrictions on building, imposed by both governments and developers, have flourished in the past 30 years, but for different reasons. Governments want to control growth and developers want to preserve values.

Therefore, depending on the neighborhood, the developer may have filed documents with the governing authority that establish certain guidelines. These are generally called the *covenants, conditions, and restrictions* (CC&Rs) for a neighborhood. Often these documents incorporate a set of architectural guidelines, which may be more or less restrictive than local building codes.

If you are selling a condominium or townhouse, the documents are called the *declaration and bylaws*. Because this type of property is typically managed by a homeowner's association, there will also be a set of rules and regulations. The association collects dues, the amount of which it adjusts from time to time, and will have a set of financial documents showing how well it has managed the condominium complex.

All of these documents should be provided to the buyer along with the title documents. They are generally recorded at the county clerk's office, obtained by the title company, and provided to the buyer. It is important for the buyer to review them. The restrictions imposed by these documents may be perfectly acceptable to the buyer. For example, some neighborhood associations will not allow anyone to have junk cars parked in front of homes and will not allow the buyer to conduct auto repairs on the property. The restrictions are designed to ensure that only certain types of people live in the neighborhood—those who like the restrictions. If the buyer happens to be a backyard mechanic, this type of neighborhood may not work.

Some associations restrict the size and number of household pets. Some condominium associations insist that anything stored on a deck (like bicycles) not be visible from the street. These restrictions and requirements should be reviewed by the buyer during the title review period. For example, an RV owner would be unpleasantly surprised to find out after closing that the covenants prohibited RVs from being parked anywhere on the property.

If you are selling a condominium, townhouse, or other property that requires the payment of dues and assessments, you should provide the buyer with the financial statements of the association. The buyer may also get copies of the minutes of the past two or three meetings. These will help the buyer determine if the association is financially viable: if it has established reserves to cover major periodic maintenance such as roofs, paved parking areas, and painting. If reserves are not substantial enough, homeowners could be faced with future special assessments. That is, every homeowner is asked to pay a set amount (sometimes amounting to thousands of dollars) to pay for a needed improvement to the whole complex. If the buyer reviews the minutes or places a telephone call to a member of the association board of directors, the buyer can also get information about what the association is planning.

These are all things that should be disclosed to the buyer in the title documents. The buyer will have an opportunity to review these documents, and it is important for the buyer to voice any objections before the stated deadline. If there is anything they cannot live with, they have the right to terminate the contract within a reasonable period of time (usually designated in the purchase contract).

Note that if you are behind in payment of any dues or assessments, the title or closing company will be notified and they will be collected from you at closing.

The Appraisal

If the buyer is having part of the purchase financed with a mortgage loan, the loan will generally be contingent on a satisfactory appraisal of value. The buyer has the option of including an appraisal contingency if they are paying cash, but it will be required by their lender if they are financing. This appraisal is the same as the one you may have had done yourself prior to determining the sales price, except that it is paid for by the buyer.

Again, an appraisal is a process whereby an experienced professional examines your home, reviews similar properties that have been sold recently, and gives an opinion of the fair-market value of your property. However, at this phase, the appraiser also looks at the contract in place between you and the buyer. If they determine the contract sets a price that is fairly close to the value established by looking at comparable sold properties, they will most likely establish a fair-market value at or close to your contract price.

If your contract price is substantially different, then the fair-market value may be either higher or lower. If the appraisal is higher than the price at which you have agreed to sell your home, you should not be too concerned, especially if you did your homework. More likely than not, you and your Realtor® negotiated a very good deal. If it comes in lower (even by $1), and the appraisal is a contingency in the contract, the contract may be eligible for termination. The contract can be kept intact, however, by one of three agreements: (1) they agree to pay a larger down payment (because their lender will only lend based on the appraised value); (2) you agree to lower the contract price; or (3) you and the buyer agree to settle someplace in between.

Financing

In most states, the buyer loses their earnest money deposit if they default on the contract, and additional penalties could be imposed. If they are financing the purchase, they will usually request a contingency for such a case. In other words, the buyer would be given a certain amount of time for the lender to approve their loan within certain established parameters. In some states, if the buyer does not have full loan approval at terms acceptable to them by the loan approval deadline, they must provide you with written notice to terminate the contract.

If the buyer is having some difficulty getting the loan they want, and a lender suggests another loan that will work, you and your agent may want to negotiate a limited extension of the contract and incorporate the new terms. Whether you agree to cooperate will depend on how interested you are in continuing to work with the buyer. If the buyer does not terminate the contract under a loan contingency and subsequently fails to qualify for a loan and cannot continue with the purchase, they are considered in default.

It is critically important that both you and your Realtor® be cognizant of all contract deadlines, as well as who must perform what obligations by each deadline. Then you will be able to protect your rights under the contract, including your right to earnest money if the contract is wrongfully terminated.

9. Preparing for Uncle Sam

> Flexible! We've bought and sold more than once using Wynne's services. Like the family doctor, Wynne is our Realtor® for life!
>
> —Ron, Kathy, Gabbi, and Gunner Glodich

Whether you're self-employed, a wage earner, or own your own business, you know that Uncle Sam, through the Internal Revenue Service, is your silent partner. It's no different when you sell your home. When you sell it for more than you paid, you create a taxable gain. However, just as you were able to take deductions on your tax return for the interest you paid while living in your home, Uncle Sam has created some wonderful tax benefits when you sell your home.

Please be aware we are *not* providing tax advice. As we said at the beginning of this book, we've tried, we really have, to be as accurate as possible when it comes to what works and what doesn't in selling a home. In this section, we will talk about how the tax laws work in your favor as a homeseller. We have attempted to ensure that everything said here is accurate and relevant, but laws change, circumstances vary, and there is always the possibility for error. Using the guidance offered here, along with your selection of a competent tax professional, whether a certified public accountant or a tax attorney, you should feel confident in selling real estate and legally avoiding or deferring taxes on any gain you may have earned. If your situation is complicated by any of a number of factors—if the property is classed as a business, farm, ranch, or multi-unit residential—please consult a tax professional who specializes in that area.

Primary Home Rollover

Let's start with the first tax advantage. It used to be that if you sold your home and purchased another, all the financial gain from the appreciation in the value of your old home could be transferred to your new one without owing current income or capital gains taxes, provided you rolled that gain over into a new home within 24 months of selling your old one. This was under Internal Revenue Code (IRC) Section 1034, prior to the Taxpayer Relief Act (TRA) of 1997. The new Section 1034 also replaced IRC Section 121, which was designed for taxpayers who were over age 55 and allowed a $500,000 exclusion for married couples or a $250,000 exclusion for a single person on the sale of their principal residence. Now you no longer need to buy another house of equal or greater value to claim the exclusion. In fact, you are no longer required to purchase a replacement of any kind. The new law simply makes your gains a tax exemption up to the 250/500 limits, and you can do this at any age. This truly makes real estate one of the best investments you can find.

You can take advantage of the new law over and over again (although not more than once every two years), but there are certain guidelines. First, both the property you are selling and the property you are buying must be your principal residence and not a second home or rental property. Second, it may be a detached house, a mobile home, a co-op apartment, or a condominium, but you cannot have more than one principal residence at the same time. Third, you must have lived in the property for at least two of the last five years prior to the sale. There is even a benefit to a spouse who is not living in the house at the time of the sale; they can claim up to $250,000 of tax-free profits, provided they too lived in the home for two of the last five years. This also applies to two co-owners who are not married, as long as they meet the occupancy rules.

Obviously, we don't want any of our clients to die, but even then these tax benefits are available. The surviving spouse, whether widow or widower, is allowed to claim the full $500,000 exclusion if the home is sold in the same year that the spouse died. Interestingly, the law allows you to purchase the replacement property up to two years either prior to or following the sale of your relinquished home.

This new Section 1034 eliminates most of the record-keeping requirements if you know that your gain will be less than $250,000 (or $500,000). By the way, the gain you are allowed to exclude is the lesser of your gain or $250,000. In other words, if your gain is $100,000 on the sale of your home, you do not get to take a $250,000 deduction. In the past, your escrow company had to file a Form 1099-S and report your taxable gain to the IRS. This is no longer required. However, if you took a loss on the sale of your home, you can't deduct that loss; remember, if you have a mortgage you have been getting an interest deduction.

Investment Property Exchanges

Tax deferral is also available when you sell a rental home, an apartment building or other investment property if you follow the guidelines in IRC Section 1031. This is called a 1031 tax-deferred exchange and is a powerful way to create wealth through real estate. You can sell investment property and transfer all of the financial gain to another larger investment property and defer the taxes that would have been due on a straight sale.

Here's how it works: An investor/taxpayer can avoid the taxes on the sale of investment property and qualify for "exchange" treatment if the property was held as investment property, or for use in a trade or business, and was exchanged from property that was like that which was sold. This is called "like-kind." However, prior to the sale of the old (relinquished) property, the seller must enter into an exchange agreement with a "Qualified Intermediary." This person or company structures the exchange transaction to meet all of the IRC requirements.

What Is a Qualified Intermediary?

A qualified intermediary is also known as a *facilitator* or *accommodator.* This is a person or company that holds the funds from your sale and structures the transaction to meet IRS requirements. Unfortunately, there are no federal or state laws that govern intermediaries or that define who can be one. Anyone can claim to qualify, however, it cannot be anyone close to you, such as your accountant, attorney, banker, employee, or family member. You must confirm that they are qualified, that they have the knowledge, experience, and credentials to perform for you. Also, they will hold your money, so you want to be sure they don't take an extended trip to a country without an extradition treaty.

Ask the intermediary if they pay interest on any funds of yours that they hold. Ask for their fee structure and whether there are extra charges if you require additional consultations. Verify that they are members of the national organization for qualified intermediaries, the Federation of Exchange Accommodators (FEA). Confirm that they carry an independent bond issued by an insurance company that specializes in this type of coverage. This is one of the most important items. You don't want to be left empty-handed if your money is stolen by the intermediary or one of their employees.

Your Realtor® should be able to refer you to one or more qualified intermediaries. Note that if you conduct a "reverse exchange" or any other type of exchange other than a straight, or "concurrent" exchange, there will be additional costs and additional rules to follow.

IRS Guidelines

There are three basic guidelines set out by the IRS to qualify for exchange treatment:

- First, the purchase price of the replacement property must be equal to or greater than the property you sold.

- Second, the debt on the replacement property, the mortgage, must be equal to or greater than the debt held on the property you sold. There should be no relief of your debt.

- Third, all of the net proceeds, the total amount you received for your property, must be used to buy the replacement property.

If you don't follow these three guidelines, you can still complete the exchange, but you may have taxes to pay. As an example, if you hold out any of the money from the exchange (this is called "boot"), it will be taxed. When attempting a partial exchange it is crucial you get competent tax advice.

Like-Kind Property

Like-kind refers to the type of property involved in an exchange. According to the IRS this is "any property held for productive use in a trade or business or held for investment purposes." As an example, you can exchange an apartment building for a commercial building, or a rental single-family home for an apartment building or a shopping center. Even raw or vacant land and a leasehold for 30 years or more count under exchange rules.

The following property is not considered real estate; therefore, it does not count as exchange property—money, stocks, bonds, and notes. Also, limited partnerships and your primary residence do not qualify.

Time Frame

Most exchanges occur as delayed exchanges, and there are two key deadlines to keep in mind. The first is the 45-day period to identify the property you want to acquire after the close of escrow on your property. The second is the 180-day period by which time you must close escrow on your replacement property. However, any exchange must be completed in the same calendar year, even if that represents less than 180 days. There are no exceptions or extensions.

You have two choices when it comes to identifying your replacement property. The first is the "three-property rule," and the second is the "200-percent rule." The three-property rule allows you to identify up to three properties that you want to acquire as an exchange. You may purchase one or all of the properties to complete your exchange as long as you follow the IRS guidelines described earlier. If you choose to purchase more than three properties, you must qualify under the 200-percent rule, which allows you to identify as many properties as you want as long as the total market value of all the identified properties is less than 200 percent of the value of the sold property. You will need to complete an "Identification Notice" for your qualified intermediary to comply with the IRS rules.

Most often, when sellers consider a tax-deferred exchange they are dealing with large amounts of money. Competent advice is suggested because the penalty for failure to follow the rules is substantial. Even typos in documents can disqualify an exchange. Please consult qualified professionals.

Buying Your Next Home

10. Buying Your Next Home

Through Wynne's Internet home search, we were able to make the home buying process a cinch!

—Brent and Tonya Easton and family

Looking Before the Sale

It is sometimes difficult to balance selling your home while trying to buy a new home. The timing is often hard to gauge. Should you wait until you have a contract before you start looking? And if you wait too long, could you face a period of "homelessness?" Don't panic. Like all other aspects of buying and selling real estate, planning is everything. Make a backup plan for what you will do if your old house is sold before you find a new one. Or conversely, make a plan for how you will deal with potentially owning two homes for a period of time. Your choices should depend on your time frame and your budget.

In general, we recommend waiting to look for your new home until you are under contract with a buyer, for several reasons. First, if you find a new home before you sell your current one you could be faced with two mortgages, which few of us can really afford—not to mention that the burden could affect the financing of your new home. Although you can use the equity in one home to finance the other, many banks will charge you a higher rate and you will have to refinance as soon as your house is sold.

Second, if the idea of two mortgages is financially unrealistic, you could get panicked and unnecessarily sell below market value. In the end, this could cost you much more than the price of interim housing. Although you could ask the seller of the home you have your heart set on to make the purchase contingent on the sale of your current home, many sellers are unwilling to do so, due to the risk it carries. This contingency could be particularly difficult to get in a seller's market, but could be much easier in a buyer's market.

Another option is to rent your house until it sells, but houses with renters are harder to sell. Generally, renters take worse care of a home, so it may not "show" as well. Buyers are reluctant to deal with the possibility of having to evict someone if the tenant refuses to leave after the sale.

It is often best to sell first and have a game plan if you don't find something right away. However, we have worked with sellers who will not even put their property on the market until they have found their replacement property. For them, it was more manageable carrying payments on two properties while they sold the "old" one rather than face the prospect of having no place to live, or moving twice.

If you cannot afford two payments or a bridge loan, you may have to make sure that you sell before buying a new property. Although potential "double moves" are expensive, you can try to lease back your sold house for a short period of time, or put your belongings in storage and stay with friends or relatives. And, of course, you can rent some form of short-term housing. Since your Realtor® knows your needs best, they can often be a very good source for finding affordable short-term housing, especially if you have children or pets. Although these choices may seem daunting or expensive, if you plan ahead, they may save you the anxiety of owning two homes. Planning ahead should include familiarizing yourself with types of homes, neighborhoods, and areas of interest so that you will be prepared to move quickly once your home is under contract.

Another rule of thumb to follow is to buy first when prices are heading up, and sell first when they are heading down. That way you are in the best position to get a good deal in the market. Like we've said before, planning is the key to making a smooth purchase or sale of property.

Safe Shopping

Once you are under contract with a buyer, it's time to find your new home. Perhaps you've been looking already, checking out homes on the Internet or going to open houses. But although you know to use a Realtor® to sell your home, now that it is your turn to buy, do you plan on using a Realtor®?

If you are like many sellers, you may be anxious to find your new home, so you have been calling on ads or For Sale signs, going to open houses, and talking to agents to whom you have been referred. But generally, you have avoided committing to one, usually on the basis that you don't want to be pressured—especially if you haven't yet sold your home. But why play the field? You've already found a great Realtor® to sell your home, and since they already know a lot about you, they may well be in the best position to help you buy a new one.

Naturally, if you had a good experience with your agent in the sale, you would want to consider working with them again. Not all Realtors® represent both buyers and sellers but it's always a good place to start, especially if you are moving in the same area.

If you are working with one Realtor® who knows you won't hop around from one agent to another, they will become as committed to you as you are to them. They will become "your" Realtor®, and they will be working for you. They will likely work to help you get qualified for financing, and when that "hot" property comes on the market, guess who they're going to call? Believe me, it won't be the person who happened to stop in for an hour last weekend, it will be the buyer to whom they are committed—it will be you. After all, you are giving them a substantial amount of business and they will want to bring to your attention any property they can find that fits your needs. If it's a great deal, all the better.

We've sold numerous properties where our buyer was the only person to see the house. We try to check new listings regularly, and also watch the newspaper classifieds for homes being sold by owners. Sometimes we see a property that is obviously underpriced, or perhaps "priced for a quick sale." It then becomes a game—get our buyer into the property before anyone else sees it, because we know it will go fast. We're off with a quick call to the buyer to let them know, "We've got one." We can usually write a contract that same day. We know the timing of each sale and we know when the buyer needs to find that new home.

We don't get paid until we produce a sale. There is not a lot of loyalty in this business, and there are a lot of short-term thinkers—people who will unknowingly lose thousands of future dollars to save a thousand today. You will find that two-way loyalty pays off. The key is selecting the right agent.

But what if you are moving to a new area and need to find a home? Obviously you need to find someone who can represent your interests as a buyer. Well, we have some suggestions. One good bet is to look for a Realtor® who holds the designation of a "buyer's agent." If your own personal agent can't represent you because you are looking in another area, we recommend having your Realtor® refer you to a top quality buyer's agent as the next best thing.

Usually when you enlist the services of a buyer's agent, you will be working with a Realtor® who will represent your interests as a sort of personal representative. This is known as an agency relationship.

Agency

When you work with a buyer's agent, you will often enter into a representation contract. A buyer-agency contract is a contract between the buyer (you) and the Realtor®, and it works two ways. First, the Realtor® becomes your agent and is obligated to represent your best interests. Second, the contract represents your commitment to the Realtor® and says that you will work exclusively with them. This agreement means that when you see a sign on a property, you will not call the listing agent yourself to negotiate a deal, nor will you go into a property that is For Sale By Owner to do the same. Instead, you will call your agent and ask them to get you information on the property. You now have an agent; use them. The whole purpose of this exercise is to get you the best deal possible. If you have selected a good agent, you should recognize they have the experience and the skills necessary to represent you effectively. It takes a modicum of trust to see that play out, and now is when your Realtor® earns their commission.

There are a few items you should pay particular attention to in a buyer-agency contract. In some states, most are already part of the standard contract, but elsewhere, this may not be the case. Before you sign, at least discuss the following topics.

Confidentiality

If you are to be represented effectively, it is imperative that the agent keep confidential any information they learn about you. In particular, your financial situation, willingness to accept concessions, and motivating factors for the purchase should not be revealed, except as a valid negotiating tool with your prior consent.

In addition, you have a right to be assured that confidential information remains confidential even after you have bought your home or after your contract with the agent has expired or been terminated in any way. If you make an offer on an inhouse transaction (where the seller is also represented by the brokerage representing you), your information should remain just as confidential as when negotiating for a property listed by another firm.

Scope of Work

The contract will contain a description of what type of property your agent is instructed to seek for you. Make sure the description fits your needs. If you are looking specifically for a residence, make sure the language limits the search to that. Do not accept language that says "any property." If you are considering purchasing a home from a family member or friend, you may ask to have that property excluded from the contract; however, you may want to ask your agent if they would handle the transaction. Pitfalls can still exist and in fact can be more serious and more heart-wrenching when dealing with someone close to you. Many close relationships have been damaged or ruined when friends and relatives have done business together. It's usually not because of a lack of good intentions, but when objectivity is lost, personal feelings get exaggerated and hurt and the process erodes. We've worked on numerous deals where family members and close friends were involved, and we have found that it becomes vitally important to ensure a win/win deal for everyone involved.

Many buyer agents typically write contracts for six months, which is a long time. Often we work with buyers of second homes, and the process involves communicating with them when they are in another city or state. We will coordinate property showings with their vacations to the area, and sometimes they buy properties we've recommended sight unseen. Even when working with locals, using a six-month representation period makes sense.

This long period can be scary. What if you decide you don't like your agent? What if your plans change? The simplest answer is to ask for a cancellation clause. Always include a clause that says that either party, the buyer or agent, may cancel the contract for any reason whatsoever by providing written notice to the other party. While they may ask for a 10-day advance notice, people who are not compatible should not have to work together. If your Realtor® is willing to give you this "out" in your contract, you can bet they are confident in their ability to represent you effectively. Keep in mind that you are not able to cancel a contract for a property on which you are already negotiating, and every contract will have what is called a "holdover" clause that entitles your agent to a commission if, after your contract has terminated, you buy a property the agent showed you.

The entire contract should be designed to be fair to both parties. It is fair to be able to cancel a contract when two people cannot work together. It is not fair to have someone do a lot of work for you and then cancel. You should be able to determine in the first or second meeting with your Realtor® whether or not you are compatible. Don't spend several weeks or months together and then decide to go with someone else.

Again, the bottom line is that if you do the same research to find a buyer's agent as you did to find your seller's agent, you should have the right person to help you find your next home (again, refer to the credentials mentioned in Chapter 2). If you are moving in the same area and can rely on the relationship with your present Realtor®, you are in a great position, but make sure your Realtor® will sign a buyer-agency contract with you. If you are planning a move out of your current area, ask you Realtor® for a referral to a competent Realtor® in your new market area.

11. Epilogue

We have bought and sold many homes in our life and dealing with Wynne was the *best*!

—Bill and Lucille Evans

Selling your home and buying a new one are two ways of improving your life. Hopefully, establishing relationships with professionals who help us throughout our lives represents another means of improvement. So many of our clients have become lifelong friends. It certainly makes the business of real estate an enjoyable occupation for us.

If you follow some of the advice presented here, we are positive that your efforts will result in similar relationships. It's often said that working with a friend can be dangerous, and certainly many good friendships are lost once an otherwise trusted friend demonstrates any level of incompetence under the guise of service. Friend or not, you are paying for professional service that should transcend a friendship. When service does not meet expectations, friendships suffer. On the other hand, when professionalism is demonstrated first, the result can be lasting friendships.

We hope nothing less for you.

Wynne Achatz
(586) 260-7653
Fax: (775) 429-0712
www.wynnea.com
sold@westrickteam.com

Doug and Kathie Whitehouse
Hannett, Wilson & Whitehouse LLC Realtors®
880 S. Old Woodward
Birmingham, MI 48009-6722
Toll free: (800) 210-9777
Office: (248) 540-8100
Fax: (248) 540-2239
doug@whitehouses.com
www.whitehouses.com

Ken Deshaies:
P.O. Box 37
Dillon, CO 80435
Phone: (888) 353-SNOW (7669)
Fax: (866) 782-6059
ken@snowhome.com
www.snowhome.com

How far will Kelly Garber go for her clients?

To the ends of the Earth, figuratively speaking. In reality, Kelly works closely with her clients, advising them on how to clear sticky title situations. If the problems are legal, she doesn't have to go far either; she can consult with one of our many staff attorneys and title professionals. At Devon Title Agency, our objective is 100% customer satisfaction.

DEVON TITLE

Oakland County Branch - 248.273.4300 DTA Online - http://www.devontitle.com
Kelly Garber direct line - (248) 594-0011

Devon Title Agency - Providing peace of mind.

APPENDIX A

Moving Checklist

8 Weeks Before Moving

- ❑ Create a "move file" to keep track of estimates, receipts, and other important information.
- ❑ Check with the IRS to see what expenses can be deducted on your next tax return.
- ❑ Start pulling together medical and dental records and ask your healthcare providers for referrals in your new city.
- ❑ Start researching your new community. The Internet is a great resource for finding chambers of commerce and community guides.
- ❑ Get estimates from several moving companies and compare them.
- ❑ Arrange to have school records transferred to your children's new school.

6 Weeks Before Moving

- ❑ Make a list of things that are valuable or difficult to replace. Plan on shipping these by certified mail or carrying them with you.
- ❑ Start working your way through each room, taking inventory and planning what to get rid of. Start planning a yard sale and find local charities.
- ❑ Choose a moving company and reserve the date of your move.
- ❑ Start collecting boxes and other packing supplies.
- ❑ Check how to obtain new driver's licenses and license plates.

4 Weeks Before Moving

- ❑ Send out change of address cards to post office, friends, subscriptions, and credit cards.
- ❑ Hold your garage sale. Donate left over items to charity.
- ❑ Contact utility companies and notify them of disconnect dates. Arrange for utility service in your new home.
- ❑ Start packing items you don't use often.

2 Weeks Before Moving

- ❑ Contact your bank and/or credit union to transfer or close accounts. Clear out safety deposit boxes.
- ❑ Confirm travel and moving arrangements.
- ❑ Return library books or anything borrowed from friends or neighbors.

1 Week Before Moving

- ❑ Finish packing! Separate essential items that you will be taking with you.
- ❑ Empty, defrost, and clean your refrigerator at least 24 hours prior to moving day.
- ❑ Cancel deliveries and services such as newspapers, and trash collection.
- ❑ Drain oil and gasoline from power equipment.

Moving Day

- ❑ Before the movers leave, check every room, closet, and cabinet one last time.

- ❑ Upon arriving, inspect everything and make sure nothing was damaged during the move.
- ❑ Keep all moving receipts and documentation in your file.

After the Move

- ❑ If needed, childproof your new home.
- ❑ Test security and smoke alarms.
- ❑ Set up all appliances.
- ❑ Get local emergency numbers and post them.
- ❑ Change the locks on all doors.
- ❑ Explore your new neighborhood!

APPENDIX B

Home Preparation Checklist

Step 1: Make Any Needed Repairs to the Primary Systems and Components of Your Home

(Unless you are selling your home "as is," buyers will need to know that your home's systems are in working order. If they are not, you should make the repairs before putting your home on the market unless you want to compensate the buyer monetarily. Take a thorough inventory and inspection of the following systems and components of your home to make sure that they are in working order. While these repairs might be costly, it will usually save you money to take care of them now rather than crediting the buyer at closing. These are items that you need to repair before you do anything else to your home if you can handle the expense).

- ❑ Make sure that your roof is in good repair. If your home has been experiencing any leaks, your roof might need to be replaced. If any shingles are loose or broken, they need to be replaced.

- ❑ Check to see that your rain gutters are flowing properly and in the right direction and are free of leaves and dirt.

- ❑ Your heating and air conditioning should be in good working order. If they are not, this can definitely cause problems in finding buyers for your house.

- ❑ Make sure that your house is structurally sound. Any cracks in the walls or ceilings should be filled in immediately to avoid further cracking.

- ❑ Check that all plumbing and septic systems are working as they should. If they are not, call in a plumber or other specialists as needed.

- ❑ Check your house for termites or any other pests. If you find any, call in a specialist to get rid of them!

- ❑ If your home has mold you should take care of it unless you are willing to sell your home for less or possibly not even find a buyer.
- ❑ Check your home for flood damage if you live in an area where flooding could be a problem.
- ❑ Radon and lead paint are serious problems that you should check for. It is best to know now rather than be surprised later on and have a deal fall through.
- ❑ If you have any broken windows, window panes, screens, or doors, you should pay to have them fixed.
- ❑ If you have any broken appliances that are fixtures and therefore will be included in the sale, such as the dishwasher, you should pay to have them fixed or replaced. Likewise, repair any broken light fixtures.
- ❑ If you have a gas stove, make sure that it works properly and that there are no gas leaks.
- ❑ Make sure all electrical systems are working properly. This includes any electrical gates, garage, doorbell, intercom, and so on.

Step 2: The Exterior of Your Home

(The exterior of your house is the first thing a potential buyer will see as they approach. Make sure that it looks neat and cared for. Use the following checklist as a guide.)

- ❑ If there are any dead or "sick" trees on your property, have them cut down.
- ❑ Your lawn should be mowed and well trimmed. An overgrown lawn can be a big turn off to potential buyers and can really detract their attention from other aspects of your home.

- ❑ Your lawn should also be green and not brown. Fertilize it if necessary and remember to keep it free of weeds.
- ❑ Shrubs, flowers, trees, and bushes should be well trimmed and healthy looking. Let buyers know that you care for your home lovingly. Well cared for greenery can give your home much added appeal.
- ❑ If you have fruit trees, make sure to get rid of any rotting fruit that has fallen to the ground.
- ❑ Rake your lawn and front drive free of drifting leaves.
- ❑ Make sure that your front walk, lawn, and entryway are clear of clutter. Get rid of any toys or bikes and store them properly.
- ❑ Hose down your front entryway so it is clean and free of dirt. If it is stained, think about covering the stain with a nice doormat if it can't be cleaned.
- ❑ If your driveway has any oil stains, clean them. Oil stains can really be an eye sore.
- ❑ If your front door looks old or worn, give it a fresh coat of paint or polish it.
- ❑ Think about placing some potted flowers by your front door. Flowers always look pretty and smell sweet.
- ❑ Wash your windows!
- ❑ If you haven't painted your house in some time and it is looking a bit shabby, you might want to consider painting it, but try to stay away from bold colors.
- ❑ Fix or replace any broken shutters, shingles, or bricks.

Step 3: The Interior of Your Home

(Most of the steps taken here will be more time intensive than anything else so follow these steps to make the inside of your home attractive and inviting).

- ❑ Organize and minimize everything in your home from top to bottom. This will involve going through every room, closet, cabinet, and any other storage area such as the garage and clearing out your belongings. You want to let potential buyers see as much clear space as possible, so this is the time to get rid of anything you no longer want or need and store the rest of your belongings neatly. You will have to do this eventually when you move, so why not start now in order to help give your home some added appeal to potential buyers? If you have so much stuff that you don't know what to do with it all, consider storing it with family or friends or perhaps renting storage space.

- ❑ Make sure that your house is clean and tidy. Clean everything in your house inside and out. Wax the floors, make sure the walls are free of dirt and smudges and dust and vacuum your furniture.

- ❑ Go through every room in your house and make sure that the furniture is arranged to make the room look the most spacious and aesthetically pleasing. Enlist the opinions of others. If you have torn, broken, worn out, or dirty furniture, you should get rid of it if you plan to do so anyway. If you can't, try covering the furniture. For example, a nice afghan over an old couch can do the trick.

- ❑ Make sure that the parts of your home that you like best are getting good lighting. Make sure that the windows are unobstructed to let in the sunlight and keep the curtains or blinds open.

- ❑ Wash the windows so they are completely clear. If any window coverings are worn or broken, fix or replace them.
- ❑ Make sure that all of your lights are working. Replace burned-out bulbs, but make sure to keep the lighting inviting.
- ❑ Clean your kitchen counters and tile so they sparkle and clean the sink. Kitchens are very important to buyers so make sure that yours is clean and bright. The kitchen is also a great place to place fresh flowers.
- ❑ Clean everything in the bathroom until it shines. Get rid of any rust stains. Hang fresh, clean towels neatly.
- ❑ Air out your house to get rid of any bad or stale odors. Try to bring in some fresh scents with flowers or a touch of vanilla.

Step 4: Updating Your Home

(If you have the time and the money, there are certain things that you can do to your home to give it added appeal and a much better selling price. There are certain things that buyers look for when buying a home, so if you do have the means, consider the following projects if they are needed).

- ❑ Remodels and updates in the kitchen are where you can get the greatest returns on your investment when you sell your home. If your kitchen is outdated and you have the means, certain updates can greatly improve your chances at selling your home for a better price.
- ❑ If your appliances are over 10 years old, replace them with new, modern appliances. Stainless steel appliances are the latest trend today.

- ❑ Old cabinets and countertops can also be replaced. If you are handy, this can even be a do-it-yourself project. Natural woods for the cabinets and granite or tile countertops can make your kitchen sparkle.
- ❑ Old linoleum flooring in the kitchen can really make the room look dingy. Consider replacing with hardwood or even tile.
- ❑ After the kitchen, updates in the bathroom are where you will see a good return on your investment in the sale price of your home. Buyers today are looking for modern bathrooms with all the latest conveniences. Glass shower doors, new tiles, flooring, and new fixtures can all give your bathrooms an entirely new look.
- ❑ If your walls are looking dirty and old, a new paint job can do wonders to the look of the inside of your home. This can be an inexpensive project that can really brighten up the rooms of your house. Choose neutral colors for a warm and soft look that will appeal to the greatest number of buyers.
- ❑ If your floors are worn and dirty, consider replacing them. Old and worn carpeting can really detract a buyer's attention from other features of your home. New carpeting can be relatively inexpensive compared with the greater return that can be obtained in the selling price of your home.
- ❑ Outdated flooring such as linoleum can make your house look retro. Most buyers are looking for homes with modern updates. If you can't afford hardwood, consider vinyl.
- ❑ Other areas to consider are very old windows and doors. Windows encompass a great deal of your home's exterior and are definitely something that buyers will notice right away.

Congratulations, after having followed these steps and preparing your house so that it looks its best, you are now ready to sell your home!

Notes

Notes

Notes

Notes